Why the Tool?

Tools have been important to the success of the human race since the dawn of time. Unlike other species, humans are adept at building and using tools to accomplish specific and important tasks. In the modern era, software tools are the latest innovation in moving humanity forward in the tools frontier. Microsoft is proud to continue to innovate and provide new software tools and contribute to an improved society for all.

The Hand-drill

The first perforated objects came from the Upper Paleolithic period and were created out of shell, ivory, antler, bone, and tooth. Typically during those times, abrasive sand under a rotating wooden stick was used to make the hole. The earliest metal drill points had sharp edges that ultimately developed into arrow shapes with two distinct cutting edges. This was an effective shape when made of lead or steel. In the nineteenth century, factory-made, spiral-fluted drills became available en masse. The point of a drill is typically conical in shape and has cutting edges where the flutes end. The angle of the point's tapered sides determines the quantity of material removed with each rotation of the drill. A drill's cutting and chip-removal efficacy is also affected by the degree of twist of the helical flutes on the bit.

WEB APPLICATIONS IN THE MICROSOFT® .NET FRAMEWORK

Based on Beta Content

PUBLISHED BY
Microsoft Press
A Division of Microsoft Corporation
One Microsoft Way
Redmond, Washington 98052-6399

Library of Congress Cataloging-in-Publication Data
Web Applications in the Microsoft .NET Framework / Microsoft Corporation.

p. cm.
ISBN 0-7356-1445-8
1. Microsoft.net framework. 2. Web site development--Computer programs. 3. Application software. I. Microsoft Corporation.

TK5105.888 .W3677 2001
005.2'76--dc21 2001030478

Printed and bound in the United States of America.

2 3 4 5 6 7 8 9 QWE 6 5 4 3 2 1

Distributed in Canada by Penguin Books Canada Limited.

A CIP catalogue record for this book is available from the British Library.

Microsoft Press books are available through booksellers and distributors worldwide. For further information about international editions, contact your local Microsoft Corporation office or contact Microsoft Press International directly at fax (425) 936-7329. Visit our Web site at mspress.microsoft.com. Send comments to *mspinput@microsoft.com.*

Acquisitions Editor: Juliana Aldous
Project Editor: Denise Bankaitis

Body Part No. X08-19536

Contents

Preface

If you are holding this book in your hands, no doubt you want information about Microsoft .NET and you want it now. You have heard about how .NET will allow developers to create programs that will transcend device boundaries and fully harness the connectivity of the Internet in their applications. You have read in the news journals that Microsoft will soon be releasing a new programming language called C# that is derived from C and C++ and is part of Visual Studio.NET. You are curious about .NET, what Microsoft has planned, and how you can be a part of it.

This book contains some of the most requested topics on Microsoft .NET available through the Microsoft Developer Network (MSDN)—Microsoft's premier developer resource. *Web Applications in the Microsoft .NET Framework* is one book in a series that includes *Microsoft C# Language Specifications*, *The Microsoft .NET Framework Developer Specifications*, *The Microsoft .NET Framework*, and *Microsoft Visual Studio.NET*. Within this series, you'll find important technical articles from *MSDN Magazine* and MSDN Online as well as subject matter overviews and white papers from Microsoft and industry experts. You will also find transcripts of key speeches and interviews with top Microsoft product managers. We have also included the documentation and specifications for the new C# language and other key documents. And code…lots and lots of code.

Who Is This Book For?

This book is for developers who are interested in being on the cutting edge of new technologies and languages. It's for developers who are eager to learn, want to stay ahead of the curve, and aren't willing to wait until everything is in place and wrapped up in a pretty package. If you fit these criteria, order a pizza and settle in—this book is for you.

What's in This Book?

This book provides an overview of Web Services, ASP.NET and ADO.NET as they fit into Visual Studio.NET and the .NET Framework. This book fully describes how Visual Studio.NET—Microsoft's next generation development environment—will allow developers to create secure and scalable applications for the Web. Once you finish this book, you'll have a fair understanding of how all these components work together, and you'll be able to write your own Web applications.

Web Applications in the Microsoft .NET Framework introduces the new features and capabilities of Visual Studio.NET. Dave Mendlen, a product planner for Visual Basic.NET, starts out by taking you through the new features such as Web Services and Web Forms and then introduces C#—a new programming language. Next up is a look at how Visual Basic.NET provides the latest object-oriented programming features. This information is followed by an article by Andrew Clinick, program manager in the Microsoft Script Technology group, on Visual Studio for Applications (VSA). This article describes how VSA can be used to customize Web Applications. Next from the .NET Show, Robert Hess interviews Mark Anders and Scott Guthrie, both members of the .NET team, about ASP.NET—the next version of Active Server Pages. Anthony Moore, a software design engineer at Microsoft, provides his insight into ASP.NET and Web Forms, including how to use ASP.NET and the Web Forms designer. MSDN's own Mary Kirtland provides a general overview of Web Services and then lays down the Web Services model for building applications. Finally Omri Gazette from the Microsoft Web Data team overviews ActiveX Data Objects as well as ADO.NET and explains how it integrates with the .NET Framework.

Some of the products mentioned in this book have since had their product name changed and officially launched after the publication of the article. For consistency sake, we've left in the original product name, but be aware that both ADO+ and ASP+ are now officially titled ADO.NET and ASP.NET.

Once you've read through the materials, don't forget to download the .NET Framework and Visual Studio.NET betas from the MSDN Web site and take them for a test drive.

A Warning

Microsoft is offering this material as a first look, but remember that it's not final. Be sure to read any warnings posted on MSDN before installing any beta products. Visit MSDN regularly, and check for updates and the latest information.

About MSDN

MSDN makes it easy to find timely, comprehensive development resources and stay current on development trends and Microsoft technology. MSDN helps you keep in touch with the development community, giving you opportunities to share information and ideas with your peers and communicate directly with Microsoft. Check out the many resources of MSDN.

MSDN Online

More than just technical articles and documentation, MSDN Online (http://msdn.microsoft.com) is *the* place to go when looking for Microsoft developer resources. On MSDN Online, you can

- Search the MSDN Library and Knowledge Base for technical documentation
- Visit an online Developer Center for resource listings on popular topics
- View and download sample applications and code, or make and review comments through the Code Center
- Participate in peer developer forums such as Newsgroups, Peer Journal, Members Helping Members, and Ratings & Comments
- Find technical seminars, trade shows, and conferences sponsored or supported by Microsoft, and then easily register online

MSDN Publications

MSDN Publications (http://msdn.microsoft.com/magazines) offers print and online publications for current information on all types of development. The following is a list of just a few of the publications MSDN produces.

- *MSDN Magazine*—a monthly magazine featuring real-world solutions built with Microsoft technologies, as well as early looks at upcoming products and new directions, such as *Microsoft .NET*
- *The .NET Show* (MSDN Show)—a regular series of webcasts about Microsoft's hottest technologies
- *MSDN Online Voices*—an online collection of regular technical columns updated each week
- *MSDN News*—a bimonthly newspaper of technical articles and columns for MSDN subscribers

MSDN Subscriptions

With an MSDN subscription (http://msdn.microsoft.com/subscriptions), you can get your hands on essential Microsoft developer tools, *Microsoft .NET* Servers, Visual Studio.NET, and Microsoft operating systems. Available on CD and DVD, as well as online through MSDN Subscriber downloads, an MSDN subscription also provides you with

- Monthly shipments of the latest Microsoft Visual Studio development system, Microsoft .NET Enterprise Servers, Microsoft operating systems, and Visio 2000
- The latest updates, SDKs, DDKs, and essential programming information

Visual Studio Enables the Programmable Web

This article was published in fall 2000 on MSDN Online. To rapidly build enterprise Web applications, developers must rely on business logic that is scalable, robust, and reusable. Object-oriented programming has emerged as the principal methodology for building such systems, and Visual Basic is now a first-class object-oriented programming language. Visual Basic.NET, the next version of Visual Basic, will offer such object-oriented programming features as implementation inheritance, overloading, and parameterized constructors. Visual Basic.NET also adds a range of modernized language constructs that simplify the development of more robust, scalable applications. These features include free threading, structured exception handling, and strict type safety, as well as productivity features such as initializers and shared members.

Introduction

To rapidly build enterprise Web applications, developers must rely on business logic that is scalable, robust, and reusable. Over the past several years, object-oriented programming has emerged as the primary methodology for building systems that meet these requirements. Using object-oriented programming languages helps make large-scale systems easier to understand, simpler to debug, and faster to update.

To enable Visual Basic developers to benefit from object-oriented design and to simplify the development of enterprise Web applications, full object-oriented language features, including implementation inheritance, will be supported in the next version of Visual Basic—Visual Basic.NET. With these new language features, Visual Basic.NET will deliver all the power required to quickly and effectively develop enterprise-critical applications while maintaining the instant accessibility that has made it the world's most popular development tool.

Visual Basic.NET will provide a first class object-oriented programming language with new features such as implementation inheritance, overloading, and parameterized constructors. Additionally, developers will be able to create highly scalable code with explicit free threading and highly maintainable code with the addition of modernized language constructs like structured exception handling. Visual Basic will provide all the language characteristics that developers need to create robust, scalable distributed Web applications with the following new features:

New object oriented programming features

- Inheritance
- Overloading
- Parameterized Constructors

Additional modernized language features

- Free Threading
- Structured Exception Handling
- Strict Type Checking
- Shared Members
- Initializers

A History of Language Innovation

The Visual Basic language has a long history of updates that map to fundamental changes in the Windows® platform. For example, the significant changes made to QuickBasic® to support Windows 3.0 GUI development resulted in the first release of Visual Basic. In Visual Basic 4.0, the shift to COM-based programming resulted in language constructs for creating DLLs. And in Visual Basic 5.0, the language evolved to support the creation of COM controls.

With each successive revision, the popularity of Visual Basic has soared. The power that the new Visual Basic object-oriented language features provide developers building enterprise Web applications will most certainly continue this trend.

Object-Oriented Programming

There are several weaknesses with traditional structured programming where data is stored separately from procedural code. Any code that is written as structured code is not modular. Because data elements are accessible from any code, it is possible for data to be modified without the developer's knowledge. This can result in runtime errors that are very difficult to debug. Additionally, maintenance can become a substantial task. Trying to understand the global impact of changing a single line of code with structured programming can be very difficult. Finally, this reliance on the programmer to manage both code and data results in much lower rates of reuse.

Object-oriented Programming (OOP) solves these problems. It packages data as well as the methods that act upon that data into a single unit called an object. An object's data can be hidden to prevent unauthorized modification. In addition, the object advertises a set of public methods to operate on this data. This concept is called encapsulation. Because implementation details are separated from the interface, the underlying programming logic can be changed at a later date without fear of breaking code that calls the object.

OOP also allows developers to reuse code and data together through inheritance. By inheriting from predefined objects, developers can more rapidly construct complex applications. Since writing new code always has the potential for incorporating bugs, reusing tested code minimizes the chances of additional bugs.

In order to address these needs, Visual Basic.NET will provide additional language features that will make it a first class object-oriented programming language with all the benefits described above.

Inheritance

Consistently the number one most requested feature for Visual Basic is support for implementation inheritance. Developing in Internet time requires rapid assembly and *massive* reuse. Visual Basic now includes full implementation inheritance, including visual form inheritance.

Developers can use the new keyword **Inherits** to derive from an existing class.

```
Class1
   Function GetCustomer()
   ...
   End Function

Class2
   Inherits Class1
   Function GetOrders()
   ...
   End Function
```

The Inherits statement supports all the usual properties associated with inheritance. Instances of the derived class support all methods and interfaces supported by the base class. And of course, the derived class can extend the set of methods and interfaces supported by the base class.

The derived class can override methods defined in the base class using the ***Overrides*** keyword. In order to reduce programming errors, Visual Basic prevents you from accidentally overriding a function; only functions that are declared "Overridable" are allowed to be overridden in derived classes.

Overloading

Visual Basic now allows function overloading, which gives developers the ability to create different versions of a Sub or Function that have the same name, but different argument types.

Overloading is especially useful when your object model dictates that you employ similar names for procedures that operate on different data types. For example, a class that can display several different data types could have Display procedures that look like this:

```
Overloads Sub Display (theChar As Char)
...
Overloads Sub Display (theInteger As Integer)
...
Overloads Sub Display (theDouble As Double)
```

Without overloading, you would have to create distinct names for each procedure or use a Variant parameter. Overloading provides a more explicit and efficient way to handle multiple data types.

Parameterized Constructors

Parameterized constructors (or simply "constructors") allow you to create a new instance of a class while simultaneously passing arguments to the new instance. Constructors are essential for object oriented programming since they allow user-defined construction code to be passed parameters by the creator of the instance. They simplify client code by allowing a new object instance to be created and initialized in a single expression.

Additional Modernized Language Features

Visual Basic.NET adds a number of additional constructs that simplify the development of more robust, scalable applications. These features include free threading, structured exception handling, strict type safety as well as productivity features like initializers, and shared members.

Free Threading

Today when developers create applications in Visual Basic, the code that they write is synchronous. That means that each line of code must be executed before the next one. When developing Web applications, scalability is key. Developers need tools that enable concurrent processing.

With the inclusion of free threading, developers can spawn a thread which can perform some long-running task, execute a complex query, or run a multipart calculation while the rest of the application continues, providing asynchronous processing.

```
Sub CreateMyThread()
   Dim b As BackGroundWork
   Dim t As Thread
   Set b = New BackGroundWork()
   Set t = New Thread(New ThreadStart(AddressOf  b.Doit))
   t.Start
End Sub
Class BackGroundWork
   Sub DoIt()
   ...
   End Sub
End Class
```

Structured Exception Handling

Developing enterprise applications requires the construction of reusable, maintainable components. One challenging aspect of the Basic language in past versions of Visual Basic was its support for error handling. Developers have found that a consistent error-handling scheme means a great deal of duplicated code. Error handling using the existing **On Error GoTo** statement sometimes slows the development and maintenance of large applications. Its very name reflects some of these problems: As the **GoTo** implies, when an error occurs, control is transferred to a labeled location inside the subroutine. Once the error code runs it must often be diverted via another cleanup location via a standard **GoTo**, which finally uses yet another **GoTo** or an **Exit** out of the procedure. Handling several different errors with various combinations of **Resume** and **Next** quickly produces illegible code and it leads to frequent bugs when execution paths aren't completely thought out.

With **Try...Catch...Finally**, these problems go away, developers can nest their exception handling, and there is a control structure for writing cleanup code that executes in both normal and exception conditions.

```
Sub SEH()
   Try
      Open "TESTFILE" For Output As #1
      Write #1, CustomerInformation
   Catch
         Kill "TESTFILE"
   Finally
      Close #1
   End try
End Sub
```

Strict Type Checking

Today the Visual Basic language is very liberal in the implicit type coercions that it will generate. For assignment and for parameter passing other than by reference, the Visual Basic compiler will allow nearly any data type to be converted to any other type by generating runtime coercion. The runtime coercion operation will fail if the value that is to be converted cannot be converted without data loss. Through the addition of a new compilation option, Visual Basic can generate compile-time errors for any conversions that may cause an error at runtime. Option Strict improves type safety by generating errors when a conversion is required which could fail at runtime or which, like the automatic conversion between numeric types and strings, is unexpected by the user.

Shared Members

Shared members are data and function members of classes that are shared by all instances of the class. Sharing a single instance of a data member or function among all instances of a class is required in a Visual Basic application with inheritance. A shared data member exists independently of any particular instance of the class. A shared method is a method, which unlike normal methods, is not implicitly passed an instance of the class. For this reason no unqualified references to non-shared data members is allowed in a shared method. Public shared members can be accessed remotely and they can be late-bound from an instance of the class.

Initializers

Visual Basic.NET supports initialization of variables on the line in which they are declared. Initializers can be used anywhere including inside a control structure. The semantics of a procedure level declaration, which includes an initializer, is the same as a declaration statement immediately followed by an assignment statement. In other words, this statement:

```
Dim X As Integer = 1
```

is equivalent to these statements:

```
Dim X As Integer
X = 1
```

Conclusion

Visual Basic is now a first class object-oriented programming language. Using Visual Basic.NET, developers will be able to create highly scalable code with explicit Free Threading. The code they write will be highly maintainable with the addition of modernized language constructs like Structured Exception Handling. Visual Basic will provide all the language characteristics that developers need to create robust, scalable distributed Web applications.

Visual Studio for Applications: Customize Distributed Applications

This article on Visual Studio for Applications (VSA) was published in December 2000 on MSDN Online. VSA is a new technology for customizing and extending the functionality of distributed applications to fit the particular needs of individual customers. This adaptability is the one issue that up to now had remained elusive to Web application developers. VSA offers an unprecedented degree of customization of middle-tier objects, a distributed engine for lightweight run time and rich-design environments, easy integration into distributed applications, all the power of the Visual Basic.NET language, and the familiar IDE of Visual Studio.NET. Web applications can be customized by harnessing the power of .NET in a familiar environment and with familiar tools. These customized applications can be run anywhere from any device. VSA is expected to be released in the same timeframe as Visual Studio.NET.

Introduction

"It is not the strongest of the species that survive, nor the most intelligent, but the one most responsive to change."

—Charles Darwin

The increasing demand for high-speed information access and the proliferation of the Internet have fueled significant changes in the field of software development in recent years. From traditional desktop and client-server applications emerged a software paradigm that allows for unprecedented levels of scalability and power—the distributed architecture. With this most recent shift in application architecture, so too came a change in the way software was delivered to customers. Today, an increasing number of applications are consumed over the Web, rather than purchased off-the-shelf of a local reseller.

Inherent in this architectural shift were new challenges to the Web application developers. Issues of scalability, performance, reliability, and security took on particular importance given the demands of Web applications. Yet while many of these issues are being addressed by prevailing Web technologies, one issue of Web application development has remained an unattainable challenge to developers—*adaptability.*

Although Web applications today provide powerful tools for managing key business functions such as Sales Force Automation (SFA), Customer Relationship Management (CRM), and electronic commerce, they do so in a way that assumes no individuality of their customers and their needs. Just as no two individuals have identical features and characteristics, no two businesses execute processes and procedures in the same way. Thus, for a Web application to truly add value to a business, it should be not only powerful and scalable, but also adaptable to the specific and ever-changing requirements of its customers.

Roots of Application Customization

This need for application adaptability, or the ability to customize applications, is by no means a new concept in software development. Microsoft founder and CEO Bill Gates first introduced this notion over ten years ago in his Byte Magazine article, "Beyond Macro Processing." In the article, Gates articulated his vision of a sophisticated and consistent development environment being integrated directly into powerful application software. Gates' vision culminated with the introduction of Visual Basic for Applications (VBA) to Microsoft Excel in 1993. VBA provided Excel with an embedded mechanism to customize, extend, and automate functionality to meet the individual needs of its customers. These rich features of VBA were soon added to other applications in the Microsoft Office suite.

In 1996, Microsoft began licensing the VBA technology to Independent Software Vendors (ISVs) wanting to deliver fully customizable desktop applications. VBA enabled ISVs to deliver an entire development platform to their customers—a feature-rich application as well as the tools to tailor it to customer needs. Customers in turn benefited from the ability to "buy and customize" desktop applications, rather than build custom applications from scratch. The "buy and customize" model provided customers with the competitive advantage needed to succeed in an increasingly dynamic business environment. Since VBA's inception, the technology has been licensed to more than 250 ISVs spanning a broad range of industries. VBA's success in the software industry is a testament to the need for application adaptability.

New Challenges in Web Application Customization

As the Internet continues to pervade society and as more and more software vendors migrate their applications to the Web, customers are offered greater application power, reliability, and scalability than ever before. However, these benefits afforded by Web applications do not preclude the need for customers to tailor these applications to their specific needs. Now more than ever, organizations must be able to adapt to the dynamic environment in which they perform their daily business operations. To succeed in this highly competitive climate, the Web applications that manage their business demand not only functionality, but also adaptability.

However, the distributed nature of Web applications introduces new challenges to ISVs wanting to deliver customizable software:

- **Location of business logic**—As software vendors migrate their applications to a distributed architecture, the application business logic is transferred from the desktop to the server (middle-tier). How can they expose these business rules such that remote developers from around the world can seamlessly and securely customize them?

- **Scalability**—Software vendors who deploy Web applications are already familiar with the issue of scalability on the application itself. With hundreds or possibly thousands of users concurrently accessing the application, it must be robust enough to handle this load without sacrificing performance. With the addition of a customization engine, this task is compounded since the custom code running against the application's business rules must also scale to hundreds or thousands of concurrent users.
- **Developer experience**—Because developers who customize the business logic of Web applications are doing so from a remote location, it is crucial that their customization experience be as seamless as possible. Regardless of the location of the Web server(s) (where the applications' business logic is stored), the developer should be relieved of the manual tasks associated with deploying, registering, loading, and debugging their custom code.

Current Customization Options

Recognizing the need for Web application customization, some software vendors have attempted to provide customization solutions as part of their applications. These options have typically fallen into one of two categories: source code distribution and service contracts.

Source code distribution describes the act of an ISV providing the source code of their Web application as part of their software offering. This option provides access to every aspect of the vendor's business logic. While this may seem beneficial at first, source code distribution often causes significant problems for both software vendor and consumer.

First, by distributing the source code of their application's business logic, software vendors lose control of their valuable intellectual property. In addition, modifying core application source code can cause problems when the software vendor releases a new version of the application. This is particularly pertinent to Web applications, which are often upgraded on a much more frequent basis than desktop applications—sometimes monthly if not weekly. Finally, because application business logic is often written in languages unfamiliar to the typical IT developer, finding the talent to customize the source code can be both time-consuming and expensive.

Other software vendors have opted to provide customized versions of their Web application through service contracts. Using these contracts, customers pay ISVs on a monthly or annual basis to provide ongoing support and customization of the Web application. Because the software vendor offering this option will typically be responsible for providing customized versions of their Web application to hundreds of customers, service contracts are often resource-intensive and very expensive.

Clearly, although source code distribution and service contracts provide some level of customization for Web applications, they introduce unacceptable tradeoffs that make Web application customization seem like an unattainable goal for many software vendors. However, the ever-increasing demand for adaptability in these applications makes customization a necessary component moving forward.

Visual Studio for Applications—Application Customization for the Web

To address the challenges inherent in Web application customization, Microsoft is introducing a new technology geared specifically for this purpose—Visual Studio for Applications (VSA). VSA is the complete solution for ISVs, ASPs, solution providers, and corporations wanting to deliver fully customizable Web applications. It enables developers to modify and extend the business logic of Web applications to fit their individual needs or the needs of their organization. Just as Visual Basic for Applications (VBA) introduced the concept of desktop application customization, VSA will extend this concept to the Web.

VSA consists of a powerful design-time environment for writing and deploying custom code and a high-performance, lightweight run-time engine for executing these customizations. VSA comes integrated as part of a Web application so that organizations can provide customers with a complete platform for developing customized solutions.

In addition, VSA uses technology that is already familiar to millions of developers worldwide. Developers write their customizations using the Visual Studio.NET IDE using the Visual Basic.NET language. The following sections describe scenarios for integrating and running VSA within a Web application and provide an overview of the features available as part of the VSA technology offering.

Leveraging VSA in your Web Application

Visual Studio for Applications was created for organizations of any size that are developing Web Applications. Whether you are an ISV developing Web applications for broad resale, an ASP deploying Web applications through a hosted model, or a corporation developing Web applications for internal use, VSA provides a fully integrated mechanism for providing Web applications that are not only powerful and scalable, but also *customizable*.

Integration

A key benefit of VSA is its integrated architecture. Unlike external tools for customizing applications, VSA is built directly into the Web application to provide seamless, secure, controlled access to the application's business logic. Integration of VSA is a two-step process that enables the organization to host the fundamental components of VSA—the design-time and run-time engines. Together, these two components, described below, provide a powerful, scalable mechanism for customers to create, deploy, and execute custom code within the Web application.

The Design-time Engine

In order to author and deploy their custom code, VSA-enabled applications provide developers with the Visual Studio.NET Integrated Development Environment (IDE). The Visual Studio.NET IDE is the premier developer toolset that offers an intelligent editor, the Visual Basic.NET language, and powerful debugging tools for developers to quickly write and deliver customized solutions.

Within the IDE, developers have secure, direct access to the Web application's middle-tier business logic. Customizations are written in the IDE using Visual Basic.NET language behind these middle-tier objects (MTOs) and are done by accessing the business logic through an object model, rather than the MTO's source code itself. This provides easy, yet controlled access to the business logic so that ISV intellectual property is preserved.

In order to provide this functionality to developers, software vendors, ASPs, solution providers, and corporations will integrate the *VSA Design-time Engine.* This engine provides interfaces that allow developers to invoke the VSA IDE on their desktop, seamlessly save and load VSA custom code, and debug their customizations.

In many cases, the VSA design-time will be integrated into a host-implemented administrative executable—typically referred to as the "administrator workbench" or the "developer workbench" (see Figure 1). These workbench applications reside on the customizer's desktop and serve as a foundation from which the VSA IDE can be invoked.

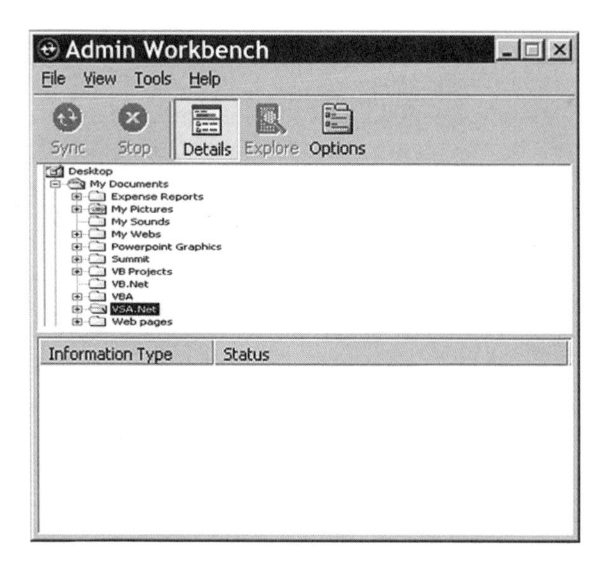

Figure 1. Developer Workbench provided by an ISV

Finally, although the VSA design-time engine enables companies to integrate the Visual Studio.NET IDE into their Web application, the integration process itself is neither cumbersome nor time-intensive. Using a set of wrapper classes provided with VSA, design-time integration can often be accomplished in under twenty lines of code (see Figure 2). This enables ISVs, ASPs, and corporations to quickly see the results of integrating VSA.

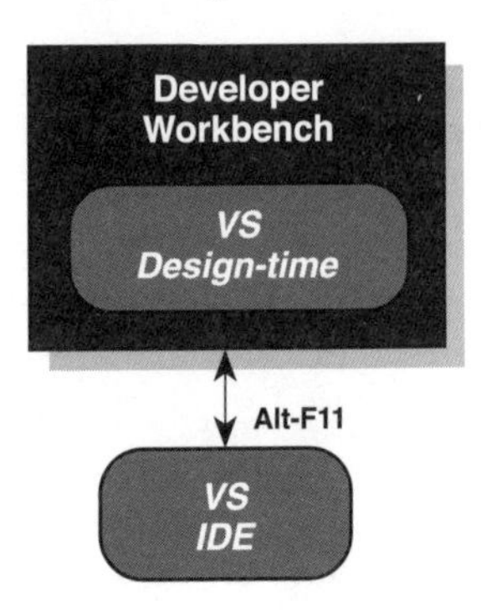

Figure 2. Integration of the Visual Basic Design-time engine into an ISV's developer workbench application

The Run-time Engine

In order to load and execute VSA custom code in a Web application, a lightweight, high-performance mechanism is required. When customers login to a VSA-enabled Web application, the VSA run-time engine is responsible for undertaking this task. ISVs wanting to integrate VSA will first expose an object model to their middle-tier business objects, then host the VSA run-time engine within these middle-tier objects (MTOs) (see Figure 3). The separate run-time engine provides a number of key benefits to developers of Web applications.

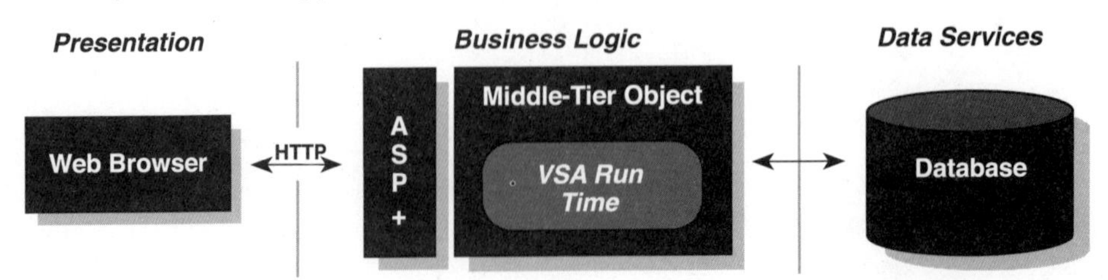

Figure 3. Integration of the Visual Basic Run-time engine into a distributed application

First, as Web applications scale to handle hundreds or thousands of concurrent users, so too should its customization technology. The VSA run-time engine was designed to be lightweight and extremely scalable on the server in order to handle the demands of today's Web applications.

Second, although it has a small footprint, the run-time engine delivers a powerful mechanism to execute custom code. It uses the same compiler as Visual Basic.NET, enabling developers to write *full Visual Basic code* behind middle tier objects to customize and extend their functionality. In addition, the run-time engine provides the flexibility to enable customizations to be loaded and executed from either their binary or source code forms.

Finally, VSA's run time support is designed to be easily integrated into Web applications. Included in the VSA SDK are run time helper classes that wrap the technical details of integration. Using these classes, VSA run time integration can be achieved in as little as three lines of code.

VSA will be available to ISVs, ASPs, solution providers, and corporations via a Software Development Kit (SDK). This SDK will provide helper classes as well as integration samples necessary to quickly and effectively embed both the VSA run time and design-time engines within a Web application.

Deployment and Execution

Once the VSA design-time and run time have been hosted in a Web application, they ship as an integrated part of the application to customers. Whether the application is being resold broadly, hosted through an Application Service Provider (ASP), or deployed internally within a corporation, VSA provides a seamless mechanism for customers to tailor and extend the business logic of a Web application to their specific needs.

When VSA-enabled Web applications are deployed to customers, the deployment typically consists of two components. The first component, fundamental to all Web applications, is the thin-client Web browser. As in typical Web applications, the browser (Internet Explorer, Netscape, etc) enables customers to logon and use the application. The second component of the VSA-enabled deployment is the developer workbench executable which resides on the developer's computer and is used to host the VSA IDE. In most circumstances, the developer workbench is not deployed to all users of the Web application, but only to those who will actually be writing and deploying customizations using VSA. These customizers of the application are typically IT staff at the ASP or within the corporation using the Web application.

To customize a VSA-enabled application, the developer will run the ISV-provided developer workbench executable and invoke the VSA IDE. Within the IDE, developers can access and customize the Web application's business logic residing on the middle-tier. A typical scenario for using VSA to customize a Web application is described below.

Customization Scenario

West Coast Sales is an ISV specializing in Sales Force Automation (SFA) applications. Like many software vendors, West Coast Sales has recently expanded their product line to include a Web-enabled version of their popular enterprise-level SFA software. One of the goals of this recent endeavor was to offer their customers all of the rich features found in the desktop version of their application, but delivered through a Web browser interface.

Although West Coast Sales is in the business of Web application development, their core competency is not in *hosting* these applications. As a result, WCS deploys their Web-based SFA application through an Application Service Provider (ASP). This ASP in turn rents the use of West Coast Sales' application to organizations wanting reliable, online access to a fully customizable Sales Force Automation application.

One such corporation, *TomRO Enterprises*, recently began renting the SFA application for use by their sales force. Although the application provides the majority of features and functionality required by TomRO, there are several aspects of the application that do not map to the organization's business model. For example, in an ideal situation, when a member of TomRO's sales force enters a new sales opportunity into West Coast Sales, the application would automatically send an email to the new opportunity thanking them for their time and expressing the salesperson's enthusiasm for working with them into the future. Because this functionality was not built into the WCS application, TomRO Enterprises decides to add it using VSA.

To do this, a member of the IT staff at TomRO brings up the WCS Developer Workbench on their computer and invokes the VSA IDE by pressing *Alt-F11*. Once inside the IDE, the developer can access the different middle-tier objects that collectively comprise the WCS business logic. Double-clicking on any of these objects calls up a code window within the VSA IDE (see Figure 4).

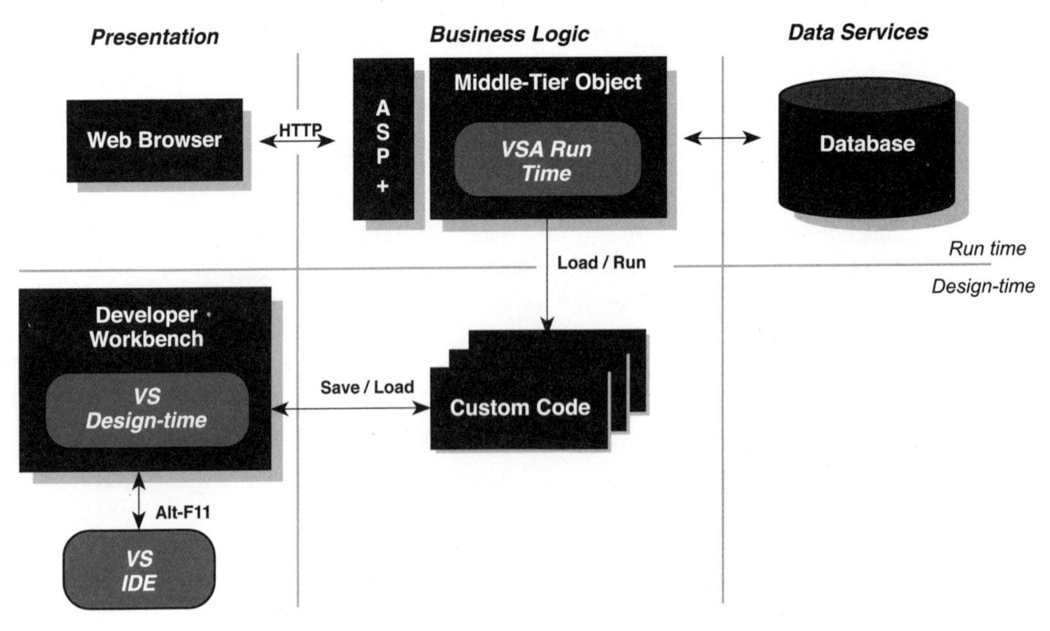

Figure 4.

Feature Overview

Distributed Engines

VSA has separated the run-time engine from the design-time engine. This split provides you with a lightweight, fast and easy to integrate engine for running your VSA customization on your applications built with Visual Studio.NET. There is no overhead of an IDE or a UI running on the server to deal with. At design time, you have the powerful and familiar Visual Studio.NET IDE to make creating your customization code in Visual Basic.NET fast and easy.

Identity-based Customization

VSA provides customization based upon specific targeted custom code. Each code item is accessed via a reference to its specific ID called a moniker. Monikers are unique to each ISV as well to the specific customization. You can set up identity-based customization on any scalable level you choose: by individual, workgroup, division, company or client.

Code Stacking

A VSA enabled application can host numerous items of custom code. These custom code items can be delivered at your choice of scoping level as well as in the sequence that you choose. By this mechanism an application can execute the customization provided for a particular company and then for each workgroup within that corporation.

Flexible Storage Architecture

VSA enables applications can persist their custom code in any location desired by the ISV. No longer is the code explicitly bound to the document. Code can be maintained in a SQL database or any data store of your choice. Code can still be maintained as associated with a document, however with the new flexible architecture, you have the choice, and are free from the traditional constraints of IStorage as in rich-client desktop applications.

.NET Infrastructure

VSA takes full advantage of all of the power of the .NET infrastructure. This frees you from having to deal with all of the minutiae of coding the underpinnings; the .NET Framework takes care of this for you. You gain from the usage of the Common Language Run time and the distributed capabilities of .NET.

Visual Studio.NET Technology

Visual Studio.NET provides a rich programming environment and all of the features developers have come to expect from a world-class development IDE. VSA, through its use of the Visual Studio.NET IDE gives you the Visual Basic.NET language, Intellisense, Project Browsers, Object Browsers, Debuggers and many more features to make your creation of custom code the easiest it has ever been.

Language-neutral Integration

VSA customization code can be run against any application built using Visual Studio.NET. It does not matter whether the application was written in Visual C++, C#, or Visual Basic.NET, your custom code can leverage the power of the objects exposed by these applications and inherit from them as well.

Seamless Deployment

No longer do you need to worry if the next iteration of your application will destroy the efforts of the VAR customizing your application. You deliver your VSA enabled application and the VAR writes new VSA custom code to be associated with it. If the custom code ever needs to be updated, there is no requirement to bring down a web site or prohibitively delete and re-install the custom code. In ideal circumstances, no re-compilation or re-deployment of customizations will be necessary; all existing customizations should continue to operate properly without modification.

Summary

Visual Studio for Applications (VSA) is a new technology for customizing and extending the functionality of distributed applications to fit the specific needs of individual customers. VSA provides an unprecedented level of customization of middle-tier objects, a distributed engine for lightweight run time and rich design-time environments, easy integration into distributed applications, all of the power of the Visual Basic.NET language, and the familiar IDE of Visual Studio.NET. Web applications can be customized harnessing the power of .NET in an environment and with tools you are already comfortable with. These customized applications can be run from any device anywhere.

Availability

A specific date has not been set for the release of VSA, however we anticipate releasing the technology in the same timeframe as Visual Studio.NET. In addition, a beta version of the VSA SDK is planned for release in Spring 2001.

For More Information

For more information on Visual Studio for Applications, please visit http://msdn.microsoft.com/vstudio/vsa.

ASP.NET: Technobabble

This is the transcript from an interview with Mark Anders, product unit manager for the .NET Framework, and Scott Guthrie, who works on the design team for ASP.NET. It was published in fall 2000 on the .NET Show on MSDN Online. During the interview the two discuss ASP.NET and how it provides an excellent infrastructure for developing advanced Web sites. Specific topics covered include the origins of ASP.NET; the new features that it offers developers; the performance of ASP.NET relative to that of ASP; the better scalability, reliability, and availability offered by ASP.NET; the greater ease in deploying applications; the extent to which ASP.NET is compatible with ASP; and migrating and caching in the ASP.NET environment.

Introduction

Robert Hess, Product Manager for Microsoft and Show Host.

Robert Hess: To continue with our focus on the .NET technologies, today we are going to talk about ASP.NET, and how this new method of dealing with server side scripting can help to increase the capabilities of your applications as Web services on the internet. But before we get to that, lets check in with Erica, and the news.

Technobabble

Robert Hess meets with Mark Anders and Scott Guthrie to discuss ASP.NET and how it provides a great infrastructure for developing advanced Web sites.

Robert Hess: If you've been paying attention to the episodes we've been having on the MSDN Show, hopefully you've gotten the idea that .NET is pretty important and that Microsoft is spending an awful lot of time and energy developing things for .NET. Well, one aspect of .NET that's come out is ASP.NET. Now, we're going to talk about the architecture of ASP.NET, deal with how it works with the whole .NET architecture and framework and developing great web sites, and stuff like that. And to assist us with that are Mark Anders and Scott Guthrie. Mark, glad you could join us again.

Mark Anders: Thank you.

Robert Hess: This is your second episode. And Scott, this is your first episode. First off, what exactly are you guys doing with ASP.NET? What does it mean to you and the company?

Mark Anders: Well, first of all, what we did was—we started on ASP.NET three years ago, actually this month is our third anniversary.

Robert Hess: Three years you've been working on ASP.NET?

Mark Anders: Three years we've been working on ASP.NET. What we started off doing was looking at ASP—which was a very, very successful platform for building Web applications—looking at it, seeing what it had that was really good and seeing ways that we could improve it. And so we spent about, you know, a year and a half really just brainstorming and coming up with ideas and then began building it, and the result is ASP.NET.

Robert Hess: Now, I guess one thing is that we recently changed the name from ASP+ to ASP.NET.

Mark Anders: Right.

Robert Hess: What exactly was the reason for that and what does it mean?

Mark Anders: Well, the reason was that the .NET initiative is really about a number of factors, it's about delivering software as a service; it's about XML and Web services and really enhancing the Internet in terms of what it can do. And the thing that was known as ASP+—and it actually had a different name when we were developing it as well—was something that was named before we had .NET; I mean it was ASP+, and we were sort of searching for a name. Once the .NET name came out, we really wanted to bring its name more in line with the rest of the platform pieces that make up the .NET Framework.

Robert Hess: The fact that it's a new version of ASP is really tied in to all this .NET Framework stuff we've been talking about these last few episodes.

Mark Anders: Yeah, exactly. The important thing to realize about ASP.NET is, it's not like we took all the ASP code from previous versions of ASP and simply ported it on top of .NET or combined it with .NET. We really wrote it from the ground up. It's a completely different code base that we spent three years working on around these new ideas and around the common language runtime and around XML.

Robert Hess: All the other .NET stuff?

Mark Anders: All the other .NET Framework technologies.

Robert Hess: Scott, what exactly do you do with the .NET then; or ASP.NET?

Scott Guthrie: So, basically, I work on the design team working on coming up with features and then working in terms of developing them with the development team.

Robert Hess: So if I was running like a blink tag in ASP.NET, you would be the person I would talk to about that?

Scott Guthrie: A blink tag, yes, that would probably be me.

Mark Anders: A server side blink tag would actually be an interesting thing.

Robert Hess: Now, so you talked about this new architecture that ASP has taken and thus got the name of ASP.NET, and you rewrote it from scratch. Now, does that mean that if I'm an ASP programmer I have to throw out everything I learned and relearn a new mindset for doing ASP.NET?

Mark Anders: Absolutely not. If you're an ASP developer, you can take all of your existing skills and very, very easily apply them to ASP.NET. If you want to continue writing in the style that you've been writing in, you can continue to do that, all of that is there. If you want to take advantage of the new features, you can do that, but you can do that incrementally and you can mix the old style of coding with a lot of the new features and take the best of both worlds.

Robert Hess: Well, what then are some of the new features that I can get access to? Why would I want to move over to the ASP.NET model?

Mark Anders: Well, there are really a wealth of new features. Number one, all of the languages are now really first-class compiled languages. So one of the things that a lot of ASP users asked for was features in VB—they wanted features in VBScript that VB had. Well, now you have full Visual Basic language. You also have lots of other languages, such as C# or Java Script or even COBOL, we've shown demonstrated COBOL working inside of ASP, so you have much better languages. You also have a much more simple and powerful page development metaphor. There are now ways to encapsulate behavior into tags so that you can get a lot of behavior simply by putting a tag on your page; you don't have to write as much code. So we've done a lot of tests where we've taken, you know, on the order of four hundred lines of ASP code and reduced it to like twenty lines of ASP.NET code. So in terms of productivity, it's much more. Web services is also a critical element. In terms of creating parts of your Web site that can be accessed programmatically by other computers.

So as an example of an XML based Web service, is taking different types of information and tying it together, like television listings and tying that together with where somebody is and creating customized television listings. Businesses are using this to allow them to talk to other businesses. So being able to easily create these XML based services is another critical piece of ASP.NET.

Robert Hess: Now, isn't that the same sort of thing that SOAP is supposed to be providing, too?

Mark Anders: Well, ASP.NET provides a very, very simple and easy way to create SOAP based Web services. It's—it is part of that.

Robert Hess: Oh, I see. Okay, so one of the aspects of SOAP is wrapping your page with all the little do-hickies that tell it what the properties method events are that your procedures expose. And so ASP.NET just automatically does this on the pages.

Scott Guthrie: Basically provides you a way that you can automate it so that it's not a page that you're building; instead we have this notion that you're building a Web service, which actually has a separate file extension. But basically within that page, you can actually define methods that you want to make Web callable and all you need to do is write your code in that page, and hit save. And if you hit that with the browser, you will actually get a listing of all of the methods that are callable, as well as a SOAP description that actually will describe how to invoke it over SOAP.

And you can either invoke it—those methods by a standard query string or you could actually go ahead and dynamically create a COM proxy object that will automate all the network traffic, all the HTTP invocation, as well as the XML marshalling to and from SOAP, that you can actually invoke this service just like you would a regular method stored in a business object located on your server.

Mark Anders: And the easy way to think about it is, in the same way that ASP, when it came out, made it really easy to write dynamic Web pages; ASP.NET makes it really easy to write dynamic Web services. And as such, you just think about the code that you want to write and the data that you want to deal with. You don't have to think about XML. Now, if you want to think about XML, you can think about XML. But you could write, for example, a method to say you give me a category name and I'll query my stock database, and my—information of my—my business, how much I have in stock, and I'll return to you a list of the products that are in that category; such as—if I'm a grocery store—milk—you ask me for milk, and I'll give you all the different types of milk that I sell. The way that you do that in ASP+ *(of course, he really meant to say ASP.NET)* is if you simply write a class in VB or C# that has a method that says get category, and it takes in the category name. It can go off and query SQL Server or any database or any XML data source, bring back the data and just return it. It doesn't have to think about actually converting it into XML; that will be done for you automatically.

Scott Guthrie: So we'll automatically handle taking an XML payload, converting it into an integer, and then if you return, say, a records set, we'll automatically handle taking that record set and serializing out into XML. So all the things that you needed to do with ASP, you know, manually parsing XML, manually cracking the, sort of, the HTTP-post content to try to get access to that raw payload, parse it, all of that is automated for you. And what we also do as part of that is we basically, dynamically, maintain for you, essentially, a contract, if you will, that explains exactly how you invoke that. So you can very easily pass this contract off to other sites and then they can then start programming directly against your site. An interesting example that one of our sites has done—and I think they are going to be guests on this show a little bit later—is they actually have come up with a list of samples for ASP+ off of their site. And they exposed a Web service that they then made available to other ASP.NET fan sites that listed all the new samples that they had written on that particular day. And so those sites can subscribe to their site and programmatically, once a day or once an hour, get a listing of all the new samples that they should go update all of their links to on their site to reference. That's an interesting way to do information application-to-application-style communication.

Robert Hess: Yeah. So it's kind of no longer talking about looking at an ASP page and a Web browser by a user; we're talking about accessing it via—

Mark Anders: Exactly. That's really the whole vision of Web services, is to realize that the Internet is really all about information. And with HTML, we've come up with a very good way to present information to people in a browser. But if you need to expose that information to other processes or other programs, whether that be, you know, a partner or other parts of your company, we haven't really had a good way to do that. And what XML is great at is representing any type of data that you want.

So you can create these services that other people can then talk to with a program, and exchange data in a very, very rich way. And it's going to really be a very powerful thing and enhances the types of applications that people can build. And long-term will also make clients richer, because clients, if they get the data as well, can do a lot more with it.

Robert Hess: And so you could even call this from an application that's not being a Web browser on the client, but being just a regular Visual Basic or C# application?

Mark Anders: Yes. Exactly.

Scott Guthrie: Absolutely. The other key thing is, because we're using SOAP and XML in open standards, one of the nice things that falls out is that we can actually talk to systems that don't have ASP.NET installed, whether they're Windows systems or Unix systems or Java-based systems, you can go ahead and communicate nicely whether you're the receiver or the sender, you can exchange information that way. So you start to see applications all around the Internet starting to interconnect in interesting ways; and as a result, you end up with much richer end-user applications.

Mark Anders: Right. It gets into another aspect, really, ASP.NET and the .NET Framework, which is really to enable applications on any type of device, and that doesn't necessarily even mean that the devices will all be running the .NET Framework. We've done a lot with direct support for things like WML in ASP.NET, so that you can easily build applications that target small devices, such as a WAP phone or phones or other small devices that handle HTML. So with a single ASP.NET page, you can target multiple devices that might have very, very different characteristics.

Robert Hess: And so the device coming at the page identifies the type of response it's wanting back out of it?

Mark Anders: Exactly.

Robert Hess: And then the ASP code identifies how to go small or large or something like that?

Scott Guthrie: Yeah. Basically, we have a special suite of servers controls, we call them mobile controls. And they automatically can emit WML or HDML or HTML depending on the type of device out there. So if you have, say, an Ericsson cell phone that might only have four or five lines of text, that goes ahead and invokes that page, we can actually automatically render an appropriate form factor for that.

Robert Hess: And does that mean that the developer of the page has to think through all the different scenarios that might come at him, like you know, here's a full color browser, here's a...

Mark Anders: No.

Robert Hess: ...Pocket PC.

Mark Anders: No. And that's really part of the magic of ASP.NET is, by having this concept of these server controls that encapsulate a lot of the functionality for you, it really gives you a nice way of encapsulating the different behavior that you expect, or the different renderings that you expect for different types of devices. And we do this in a lot of different scenarios; for example, we have a set of controls for doing validation, which is a very, very complicated thing to do in a Web site, especially when you want to, you know, emit script code that goes down to the client and does the validation; you also want to have server-side validation for down level browsers. And we have a set of controls that will automate all of that for you. So they encapsulate the basic validation behavior, yet, if it's a rich browser, they will emit one thing, they'll emit—script code. And if it's a down level, they'll run the validation and produce the exact same experience, except it's happening server-side, for those down level browsers.

Scott Guthrie: And it will also automatically handle scenarios where clients that deliberately try to go around client-side script or deactivate client script and spoof things, it will trap those as well. And all you need to do is drop these on your page, declaratively as tags, and you can write two or three line of code against them, and you actually have a fully validated page.

Robert Hess: You just basically identify, you know, this is the form this number is supposed to be in—

Scott Guthrie: Exactly.

Mark Anders: Exactly.

Robert Hess: Phone number, zip code, something like that and just—

Mark Anders: Yeah. There are a whole bunch of them. There's ones that say, you know—they just have to fill in something or they have to fill in something that matches this regular expression or they need to fill in a number that is within this range or they need to—you know.

Scott Guthrie: And they're extensible, so part of our framework is really enabling third parties to do interesting stuff. So one of our third parties has actually come up with a zip code validator. You just drop it down on the page and point it at a text box and it will validate whatever number you type into that text box is a valid zip code. So then you can have very type specific scenario driven validation. It just makes writing pages a lot, lot easier.

Mark Anders: Scott actually touched on the things that are sort of new in ASP.NET. And really the complete componentization of the system and allowing developers and third parties to plug in, literally, at any level of the system, is the other big innovation. One of the things that we heard from people with ASP a lot was: I love ASP, I love this Session State thing, but I wish it worked in a Web farm, for example; how can I make it work in a Web farm. And the answer was, well, you can't. With ASP.NET, number one, we've made Session State work in Web farm, so you're taken care of there. But if you actually want to completely replace our implementation of Session State, you can do that. If you would like to modify the way we do output caching in ASP.NET also has output caching; you could easily do that, because the entire system is componentizied.

People's—other people would say: We love things like the response and the request and the session and the application, but we really want to write, kind of, more at the ISAPI level, how can we do that. And the answer was, well, all of those things are built into ASP and there's no way to drop down to that low level. With ASP.NET you can.

Robert Hess: Now, when you say ISAPI I remind you there's essentially two different styles of an ISAPI application; there would be an ISAPI application and an ISAPI filter—

Mark Anders: Yes.

Robert Hess: —which solve two different problems. Now, I can imagine how ASP.NET could take care of the ISAPI application model. Does it also do anything with an ISAPI filter?

Scott Guthrie: Yes, it also—we also support what we call an ASP module extensibility point, and it basically allows you to do ISAPI filter like functionality. So some common examples of that, like Mark mentioned, replacing Session State is actually done at that level. Doing things like URL rewriting. A common scenario that a lot of customers have asked for is they want to personalize a URL for a client, let's say a financial institution; so they can give you a URL that looks friendly. You know, www.financialinstitution.com/scott, but they don't want to create a view route. So they want to do some very fancy URL rewriting techniques, you can do that.

Robert Hess: So the URL comes with "/scott" in it, the ASP.NET actually switches around and goes wherever it's—

Scott Guthrie: Right. So you have some code, that right before the actual page executes, basically strips out the "/scott" part and actually executes a common page, that's really common across all the users and then personalizes in that way; rich things like that. And so there's a module API that you can plug into to take advantage of that.There's also an extensibility point that we've extended so that—with ASP we have this notion that we call Global.asa, and so there was a notion of an application start and an application end event, and a session start and session end event. We actually allow you to tie into that ISAPI filter like functionality from within that Global.asa. So if you want to go ahead and do that URL rewriting, you don't even need to write a module, you can actually just do it within your Global.asa.

Mark Anders: And one of the places we do—we've done a lot with security and allowing really flexible authentication. So in the past, with ASP, you used IIS's built in authentication, which meant you authenticated against the NT SAM. With ASP.NET, we actually plug in security modules in that filter-like part of the request processing, and they can fire an event—for example, say on authenticate. So if you want to do forms-based authentication where you go out to a main frame or some database that you have of usernames/passwords and do the authentication yourself, you can just write that in the global.asa or, you know, within a component that syncs with that event.

Robert Hess: So I can write my own database of user names—

Mark Anders: Exactly.

Robert Hess: —and have the standard authentication go against that.

Mark Anders: Yes, exactly.

Scott Guthrie: And if you chose to, you could even make that even a little bit richer, which is not only have user names and passwords, but also have a notion of roles. So you could actually map those users into roles. And so you could actually architect your site so that you could say, rather than ACL, oh, yes, you know, Joe and Mark have access to this particular page. Instead, you can actually ACL that page to say power users have access to that role or to that resource. Or premium accounts have access to this part of the site. And then what you could actually do inside your database is basically tell us, you know, yes, the user name and password for Mark matched, and by the way, here are the set of roles that he belongs to; and then our security system will take care of the rest, in terms of guaranteeing that he has access to those pages or services. And the key thing is all this architecture, the security architecture, the caching architecture, works for both pages as well as for these XML services that are new.

Robert Hess: What about from a performance standpoint, all this stuff being added, all these capabilities—I mean, are we seeing better performance?

Mark Anders: We're actually seeing much, much better performance. When we formed the ASP.NET team, the second developer that we had on the team was actually a guy who did performance work. And what he was doing—we were working with very early versions of the common language runtime—he was really investigating every operation and what was fast, what was slow; working with the runtime team to speed up the things that were slow, and pointing out performance problems. And the result is that we are much, much faster than ASP. First of all, all of the code is compiled. So it compiles down to native code, it's no longer interpreted.

Robert Hess: Okay. The ASP code itself that I write as an ASP.NET programmer isn't interpreted?

Mark Anders: Correct.

Scott Guthrie: The nice thing is you still maintain the sort of—I can still write my code in the file and hit save. It's just instead of parsing that and passing it off to a script engine to interpret it at runtime; we instead parse that, pass it off to a compiler, and then use common language runtime. At runtime, we're actually executing native code. So you have basically C++ level performance out of your VB code now.

Robert Hess: So when does that compilation—does it happen when I'm—when I save the file out and the NT file says notices of file change or the first time the page is—

Mark Anders: Exactly at the same time that it happened with ASP, which is when somebody requests the page. We actually notice whether we have it compiled, and if not, we'll compile it. Now, we do a lot of more interesting things in ASP.NET to actually make compilation much more efficient so it appears to you as fast as ASP did. You know, you used to save an ASP page and you request it and suddenly it's there.

It feels even faster in ASP.NET, even though it is compiled. But since we are compiling it, for example, if you reboot the machine and restart or you shut down the Web server or you shutdown the process—and I maybe talk a little bit more about the things we've done to make the machine more reliable, as well—but we don't have to re-compile that page again. We can detect that it's already been compiled and just load it, so it's actually much, much faster and more scalable.

Robert Hess: And that's because of keeping it in a cache somewhere, a private cache that's hidden?

Mark Anders: Yes.

Robert Hess: And so I don't have to have a .ASP file, an OBJ file, and an EXE file and junk like that.

Mark Anders: Correct.

Robert Hess: Okay. So you mentioned about performance.

Mark Anders: Well, we were talking about performance. And, yeah, across the board performance is much better. We've also done a lot for scalability and reliability and availability. So one of the assumptions that we made was that, even though we have the common language runtime, and I think you had a session on the common language runtime that talked about all of the stuff that it does to make applications more reliable.

Robert Hess: Right.

Mark Anders: Such as really strong type checking; a managed environment—that means that if you try and override an array, you'll throw an exception rather than just trashing memory. But even in addition to all of that, we build in reliability mechanisms above and beyond that. So, for example, we can detect, obviously, a crash, but also memory leaks that spiral past a certain point. We can detect deadlocks, you can even configure it so that your application just restarts every once in a while.
So we'll fire up a new instance of the application once an hour or once a day or once every two thousand requests or something like that, and then allow the old one to finish processing the requests that it's processing and then have the new one take over.

Scott Guthrie: Well, keeping as part of this reliability mechanism is that you don't have any interruption of service to your clients. So what will happen is we'll actually spin up dynamically a new process, start sending new request to it, let the old process complete all the requests it's currently processing, and then we will delete the old process. So as a result under the covers, the system is doing reset, effectively; but without any administrator intervention; but your customers just think, oh, the server is still there, everything is working. But as a result you get much, much higher reliability.

Mark Anders: Another thing that that's all predicated on is getting back to this idea of Session State. And Session State no longer needs to be running in the same process as your code is running in. It can run as a service on that machine, or for a Web farm scenario you can run it on a different machine that multiple front end machines on your Web farm can share.

Robert Hess: So you would still have on one machine; is this the Session State existing?

Scott Guthrie: No, it's actually possible to have the Session State on the—

Mark Anders: Multiple.

Scott Guthrie: Stored on multiple machines and then have multiple front-end web servers actually go ahead and access those state stores.

Robert Hess: So if I'm a user and I'm accessing a machine and hitting one Session State on this machine, if my next access comes up to another machine, the data in the Session State is shared?

Mark Anders: Well, the way it typically works in a web farm scenario; say you're a user and you come in to machine A and then you come back a little while later and you hit machine C, is that you would have the Session State on a separate machine, and that Session State could either be running in our Session State provider or it can even be running within SQL Server. We have a way for SQL Server to be the server of the session information. But both of the front-end machines, as many as you have, get access to that same Session State.

Robert Hess: That's where you're sharing data, then, from that standpoint?

Mark Anders: Yes, exactly. But you can imagine that once you have that Session State, out of the process that's actually running the ASP, if it crashes, if we shut down your code, we detect some type of resource leak or a lockup or anything where you've configured it to just restart once an hour, all of your sessions are still safe.

Robert Hess: Because they're stored on this separate machine?

Mark Anders: Right.

Robert Hess: Right.

Mark Anders: And if you even have just a single machine, you can take advantage of this; you can run it out of process with the process that's running your code, so that, you know, as though processes even just come, they can just access the Session State that is a safe protective process.

Scott Guthrie: So as Mark mentioned, the big benefit of this is: (1) reliability. You don't have the perception of your app ever going down or a user's data ever being lost. The other big benefit is now, suddenly, your app is no longer tied to a single machine. If you use Session State, you can now actually scale your app out across multiple machines, and as result, there's really no upper bound, in terms of how big or how many users your app can go ahead and service.

Robert Hess: So it sounds like we have two different things going on here, one, we have is that ASP.NET has a lot of new functionality and new capabilities you're exposing that people take advantage of. And the other is that under the covers what ASP or ASP.NET are doing for you have a lot of additional features and capabilities that just make it that much better.

Mark Anders: Yes.

Robert Hess: Which to me says if I've got an existing ASP Web site, if it's working perfectly fine for me, I don't need to make any changes to it; just upgrading and using ASP.NET as the provider of the underlying framework—or something like that—is going to make my Web site that much more robust.

Mark Anders: Well, that's actually a very, very interesting point, because one of the things that we wanted to make sure was: If you are that user and you say my app is running just fine, I don't really want to make any changes, and let me just install this ASP.NET thing on my machine. Well, if you do that, we're—we don't actually replace ASP on the machine. So ASP and ASP.NET can run side by side on the same machine. You would actually have to explicitly move it over and configure your machine. It wouldn't be hard to do, but you would need to tell us that you want ASP.NET to be running these applications. Because you can imagine that on a box that's hosting multiple applications, if you install this new application environment, with it's compilers and all of this new .NET stuff, maybe not every app just upgrades flawlessly and gives you exactly the same performance. People who do server side programming spend a lot of time tuning their application, making sure that it really works. And we wanted to not give anybody rude surprises. So ASP and ASP.NET run side by side, and so you would actually need to—

Robert Hess: Actually manually touch something to bring that up.

Mark Anders: To say, use this.

Robert Hess: But if I did do that, if I did take and say, okay, let's install ASP.NET under the covers, and let's mark my files, and say these are now to run the ASP.NET environment. Even if I didn't make any other changes to the files at all, I would probably get a much more robust and scalable solution.

Scott Guthrie: Yeah, you would get a more robust and scalable solution. The thing—I think it is important to mention, though, is that we're not a hundred percent compatible with ASP, we're very, very—you know, we're relatively close, but there have been times over the last couple of years, as we are developing the platform that, for one reason or another, we've had to break some compatibility; some of those people won't notice at all. The order of which we get cookies has actually changed slightly. Some of them are more dramatic. And so just to set expectations, it's not a hundred percent compatible. So the important thing is your existing code and your existing pages will continue to work just fine if you install ASP.NET.

Robert Hess: And if you choose then to upgrade it to—to use ASP.NET, you want to make sure you do testing to verify.

Scott Guthrie: Yes. And there will probably be some things that you need to go ahead and fix up.

Robert Hess: Okay.

Scott Guthrie: Now, for the most part those are, hopefully, relatively small things that you need to change, and we will have some automated tools to help you to do that. But you probably will, on any kind of any large app, you would almost definitely have some changes that you're going to want to make.

Robert Hess: Okay. And then let's say you wanted to take the jump and actually go to a full blown ASP.NET thing, are there any key aspects of understanding the architecture of your application you might need to rethink, or is it just simply looking at what some of these new things are and taking advantage of them?

Scott Guthrie: Well, that's an interesting part. There is sort of migrating, which is taking a page or taking your skills that you have today, and you can certainly do that, and just writing, you know, using ASP.NET, you can get much better performance, using the exact same skills, exact same techniques that you do. Something that I recommend to people when they start looking at the platform is to play around with all the features, because in addition to sort of migrating, a lot of times I think people—it's sometimes worthwhile stepping back and saying well, actually, there's all these new features; rather than just migrate, maybe I should actually re-architect a little bit. You know, this validation that we mentioned earlier in the episode. Most apps have some degree of validation. You can keep your existing validation logic and it will just get faster in ASP.NET, but it might make sense to actually rip yours out and actually use our validation components instead. A lot of people have their own sort of security architecture that they built with ASP, where they have sort of an HTML sign-in page. They might actually decide to say well, actually, rather than use my own technique and use Session State to keep track of who the user identity is, I might actually want to use the built-in form space authentication that comes with ASP.NET.

Caching is something else, in terms of performance, that we didn't mention earlier. A lot of advanced developers go ahead and have actually come up with very good techniques to try to figure out, how can I cache results, parts of a page or an entire page on a server, so that when two browsers request the same particular resource, I don't have to regenerate both; I can just used the cached version of the second one. On ASP.NET we have built in caching support. So all those terms sort of features that up. And it's worthwhile spending—before you just blindly start playing with it—is actually worth playing around with the quick starts. We have about nine hundred samples that we ship as part of the SDK, it has a large number. We also have some great end-to-end applications that we ship, an e-commerce app, a portal framework app for billing like an intranet portal. It's worth, actually, playing around with those and looking at how they're architected, because I think you'll find there's a lot of tips and tricks that you can pick up, and dramatically reduce the amount of code you write. And also the code you do end up writing becomes a lot cleaner. And I think you're going to find that, you know, suddenly that fifty lines of that real unmanageable code, becomes about five or six lines of really clean code, that when you come back a couple weeks later and look at it, you'll know immediately what it does.

Robert Hess: That would be amazing. I'll come back to code sometimes and say what was I doing. Well, thanks a lot Scott and Mark. Mark, did you have any closing comments you want to have? Scott had the little last bit about what he thought was important.

Mark Anders: Well, I guess really to sort of zoom up to the 50,000 foot level, the key things about ASP.NET are that, number one, it makes developers a lot more productive. It makes applications and systems more reliable. We didn't even talk about the deployment stuff. And there's a whole bunch of stuff that make applications really easier to deploy. So for example, if you copy a DLL while your application is running, it's not locked any more. You know, your application will, actually, gracefully migrate to the new version. I mean, there's a whole host of stuff and really improving performance, reliability and availability and scalability; I guess, all of the abilities, are really the key, top level things. Beyond all of that, there's just a tremendous amount of new features. I know a lot of people who have seen the progression from ASP 1.0, to 2.0, to 3.0; are saying oh, there are now three new methods on the server object or the response object or something like that. This is, you know, just a tremendous wealth of new features. And Scott and I, I think, have done hundreds of presentations over the last three years of ASP.NET, and I remember saying to him after the first month, "our winning streak can't continue forever," but up until this point it has. And as, you know, we've gotten it out into the hands of literally hundred of thousands of developers and the enthusiasm has been really incredible.

Scott Guthrie: I think it's best summed up with a comment that a few advanced developers made to me at a conference recently which is: This makes Web development fun again, which is something that, you know, they've been thinking of as sort of a job for the last two years. This is something that's really new that makes their life, you know—makes developing a lot easier, but also just makes it a lot of fun to build apps.

Robert Hess: A lot of fun and a good way to make money.

Scott Guthrie: Yep.

Robert Hess: Okay. Well, thanks a lot for joining us. It's very much appreciated. And I'm sure we'll probably see you back here again sometime.

Mark Anders: I hope so.

Robert Hess: Well, that covers the architecture segment about ASP.NET.

ASP+ and Web Forms

In this article, Anthony Moore of Microsoft Corporation discusses the process of getting used to using ASP+ and the Web Forms designer. The article was published in September 2000 on MSDN Online. For Microsoft Visual Basic users who are not familiar with Web development, the Web Forms designer with ASP+ is the easiest way to begin. Web Forms does a great job of making Web development seem like GUI development, but there are some key differences between the two. Developers will notice these differences when they first try to declare and use a member variable, add a control at run time, pass data from one page to another, or use data binding.

The Skills You Already Have

If you are a Microsoft® Visual Basic® user who is not familiar with Web development, the Web Forms designer with ASP+ is the easiest way for you to start. Overall, the process of using controls, properties, events, and data in ASP+ is not too different from writing Windows applications using Visual Basic 6.0 or earlier. By comparison, ASP and other Web development environments are very different indeed, and shifting from one to another can seem like the programming equivalent of learning to walk again.

By now you may have seen a Web Forms demo or gotten your hands on some bits and tried this out. Usually, the first thing you will try with Visual Studio will go something like this:

1. Create a new Visual Basic Web application.
2. Drop a Button control and a Label control on the page.
3. Double click the button to get an event handler.
4. Change the Label text to “Hello World!”
5. Run the project.

Here is how your first ASP+ page might look in the Web Forms designer:

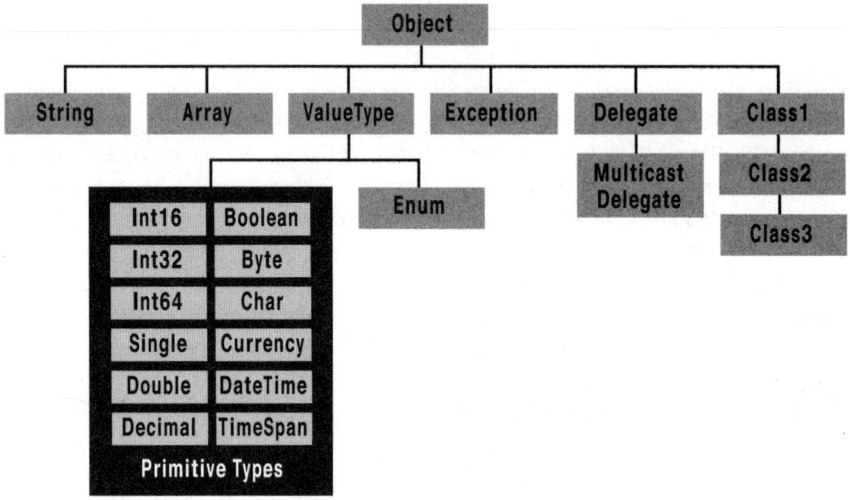

Figure 1. An ASP+ page in the Web Forms designer

I don't know about you, but the first time I did this my feeling was "This beats the stuffing out of ASP or CGI scripts. This is easy!"

As with creating Windows applications, creating a reliable and scalable Web application is extremely complicated. Our hope for ASP+ is that it hides most of this complexity from you just as Visual Basic 1.0 did for Windows development. We also want to make the two experiences as similar to each other as possible so that you can "use the skills you already have."

You Can Mostly Use Those Skills...Mostly

Web Forms does such a fantastic job of making Web development seem like GUI development that it can lull you into a false sense of security. However, there are some very fundamental differences between the two, which, if you're not aware of them, will lead to some common mistakes when you get started.

You are probably in for a bit of a shock when you first try to do the following:

1. Declare and use a member variable.
2. Add a control at run time.
3. Pass data from one page to another.
4. Try to use data binding.

Shock Number One: Page Lifetime

Let's take our page and put a counter for the number of times the button has been pushed:

```
Private myCounter As Integer
Protected Sub Button1_Click(ByVal sender As System.Object,
        ByVal e As System.EventArgs)
    myCounter += 1
    Label1.Text = myCounter.ToString()
End Sub
```

This looks like it should work, but if you try out the page you will find that the counter never goes above one.

When doing simple scenarios with control events and properties, it will probably seem like the page and the controls are created and hang around for as long as the user is playing with them. Even as an experienced Visual Basic user, when I first started using ASP+ I had a couple of questions about the page lifetime, such as:

- How long does the server hold onto a page before throwing it away?
- Doesn't having all those objects use a lot of memory on the server?

The answers to those questions are "0 seconds" and "no," respectively. The page and its controls are created and then completely discarded every time the page is accessed. The only instances of the **Page** class in memory on the server at any given time are those being processed for a user request at that particular instant.

One of the great technical accomplishments of ASP+ is that it is able to preserve most states on a page between round-trips to the server, and without keeping the pages in memory. However, it does not automatically preserve absolutely everything, so if you declare a new member variable it will be discarded unless you have saved it explicitly. It should be clearer now why the counter example did not work as expected.

Here is a version of the event handler that works effectively:

```
Protected Sub Button1_Click(
                    ByVal sender As System.Object,
                    ByVal e As System.EventArgs)
    Dim myCounter As Integer
    myCounter = CInt(State("myCounter"))
    myCounter += 1
    State("myCounter") = myCounter
    Label1.Text = myCounter.ToString()
End Sub
```

The **State** object is a collection of objects on the **Page** class into which you can put values and have them saved between round-trips. This becomes part of the page's view state, a collection of information that actually is written into the HTML in a hidden field. Controls that have had their properties changed at run time also make use of the view state to restore those values when the page is processed again.

A cleaner way of having a persisted value is to define a formal property:

```
Private Property myCounter() As Integer
    Get
        Return CInt(State("myCounter"))
    End Get
    Set
        State("myCounter") = value
    End Set
End Property

Protected Sub Button1_Click(
                  ByVal sender As System.Object,
                  ByVal e As System.EventArgs)
    myCounter += 1
    Label1.Text = myCounter.ToString()
End Sub
```

You can actually put reasonably complex objects into **State** and still have them persisted. Apart from simple types, it is possible to store many of the container types defined by the common language runtime, such as **ArrayList**, **Hashtable**, and **DataSet** objects.

Salvation Is Not for All

The reason things can be confusing is that much of the data is saved between round trips, but not everything. A quick summary of what is saved and what is not follows.

Saved:

- Page properties
- Properties of controls declared on the page
- Data in data-aware Web controls such as Repeater, DataList and DataGrid

Not saved (unless you save them yourself):

- Variables and properties you add to your **Page** class
- Events handlers hooked up in code rather than being declared
- Controls added or deleted in your code
- Rows and cells added to tables in your code
- Any changes made during rendering

We have already seen how to work around the first problem by using the **State** property on the **Page** class. In order to understand the rest, it is important to have an overview of what happens when a page is processed.

Page Processing Sequence

Here is roughly what happens when a page is processed:

1. Page and controls are created.
2. Page and controls state is recovered from view state (post-back only).
3. Page controls are updated based on user input (post-back only).
4. Page is validated (post-back only).
5. Events fire.
6. Page and controls state is saved into view state.
7. Page and controls are turned into HTML.
8. Page and controls are discarded.

Page and controls are created. Every time the page is processed, including the first time, it is created along with its controls based on the contents of the ASPX file. The very first time the ASPX file is accessed by anyone after being modified it will actually be turned into generated source code and compiled into a DLL. As a result, page access is very fast because there is no parsing going on, just execution of compiled code. This generated code creates controls, sets properties, and hooks up events.

Page and controls state is recovered from view state (post-back only). If any controls declared in the ASPX file have been changed in code you have written, the changes made are written out in the view state. For round-trips after the first access, these changes are reapplied to the existing controls. This is why properties stay the same between round-trips, but more complex changes such as adding events or adding controls do not.

Page controls are updated based on user input (post-back only). Server-based input controls have their properties updated. In ASP you had to manually update input controls to make them remember user input such as this. Because this step occurs before most events fire, you can always query control properties such as the TextBox and get the value that the user entered.

Page is validated (post-back only). If you are using validation controls, they are evaluated at this point. Again, because this occurs before most events are fired, you can reliably check the validity of the **Page** object or individual validators.

Events fire. This is where code you have written is executed. The first event to fire is Page_Load. This event is then followed by events related to changed data, such as the TextChanged event on TextBox. Finally, the event related to the action that actually caused the page to post-back is fired, such as the Click event of Button. The very first time the page is accessed, Page_Load is usually the only one of these that fires.

Page and controls state is saved into view state. Any changes to declared controls are saved into the view state. Changes made after this point, such as any code that executes while rendering, will not be saved into the view state.

Page and controls are turned into HTML. The first sub-step is called the *pre-render* where controls do any additional steps required before rendering. Because it happens after all other events, overriding the **PreRender** method on the **Page** class is actually a useful way to have code that executes after all other events but before rendering takes place. The next sub-step is the *render*, where the HTML is actually generated. Some events such as the DayRender event of Calendar are actually executed while this is going on. Also, for ASP compatibility, any code inside <%...%> blocks is executed at this time.

Page and controls are discarded. The common language runtime is very efficient at creating and discarding small objects, so there is no significant performance concern with all this objection creation and deletion.

Having this sequence for page processing may seem convoluted compared to GUI development. However, this process of minimizing object lifetime makes it possible to create Web applications that are very fast and scale to large numbers of simultaneous users.

Knowing this sequence should help you work around various issues. For example, the sequence explains why changes to objects made during rendering are not persisted. In the case of dynamically adding events, you will want to add them in Page_Load so that they will always get hooked up in time. Dynamic controls are a little trickier. We'll look at those next.

Shock Number Two: Adding Controls at Run Time

Let's say you want to dynamically add rows to a table. You must drop a Table control, a TextBox control, and a Button control onto a page using the designer, as seen in Figure 2:

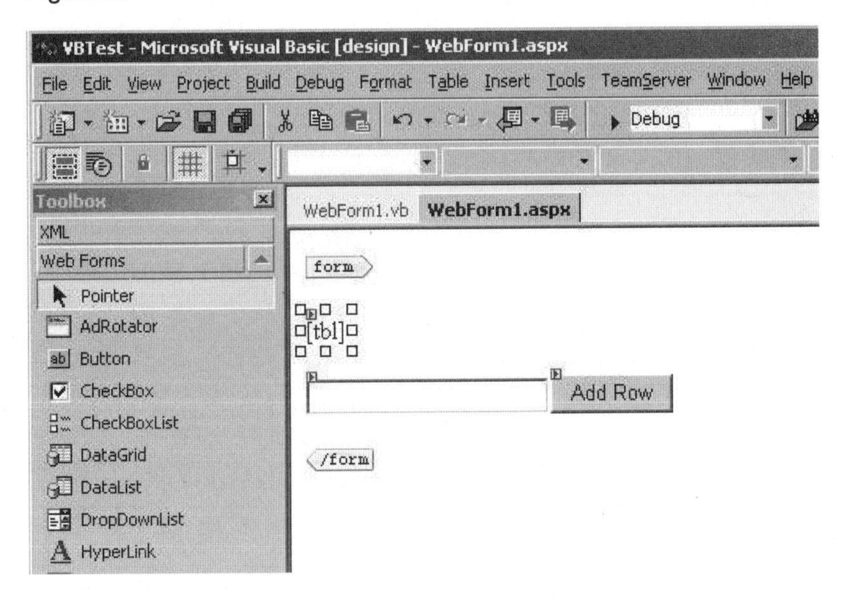

Figure 2. Web Forms designer with Table, TextBox, and Button controls

When the button is clicked, we want the contents of the TextBox added to the rows of the table. You might reasonably expect to accomplish this with the following code:

```
Public txtRow As System.Web.UI.WebControls.TextBox
Public cmdAddRow As System.Web.UI.WebControls.Button
Public tbl As System.Web.UI.WebControls.Table

Protected Sub cmdAddRow_Click(
           ByVal sender As System.Object,
           ByVal e As System.EventArgs)
    Dim cell As New TableCell()
    Dim row As New TableRow()
    cell.Text = txtRow.Text
    row.Cells.Add(cell)
    tbl.Rows.Add(row)
End Sub
```

However, because controls are not persisted automatically between round-trips this will not work the way you might expect. It will always result in a table with a single row because the table is being re-created on every round trip. If you are creating controls dynamically, you need to keep track manually of enough information to recreate them fully every time. In the preceding example, you would need to at least remember the list of strings. A version that works by storing the strings in the view state follows.

```
Protected Sub Page_Load(
           ByVal Sender As Object,
           ByVal e As EventArgs)
    Dim s As String
    For Each s In RowTexts
        AddARow(s)
    Next
End Sub

Private Sub AddARow(ByVal s As String)
    Dim cell As New TableCell()
    Dim row As New TableRow()
    cell.Text = s
    row.Cells.Add(cell)
    tbl.Rows.Add(row)
End Sub

Private ReadOnly Property RowTexts() As ArrayList
    Get
        Dim o As ArrayList
        o = CType(State("rowTexts"), ArrayList)
        If IsNothing(o) Then
            o = New ArrayList
            State("rowTexts") = o
        End If
        Return o
    End Get
End Property

Protected Sub cmdAddRow_Click(
             ByVal sender As System.Object,
             ByVal e As System.EventArgs)
    RowTexts.Add(txtRow.Text)
    AddARow(txtRow.Text)
End Sub
```

Note that because of the order of events it is necessary to add the row in both the Click event and Page_Load. This is how it looks at run time:

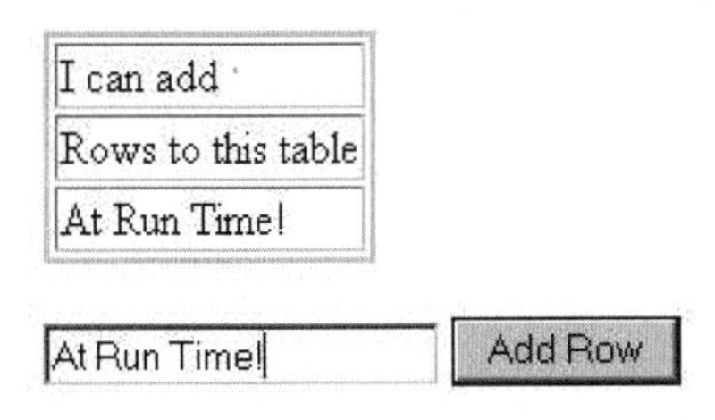

Figure 3. Table with row added at run time

While this example concentrates on adding to a table, you face the same issue with any controls that are added or deleted at run time. And, while you can add controls directly to the page, they probably won't go where you would expect. To position a control at run time you need to at least declare the parent control in which you want to put it. The Panel control is good for use as a container control.

If all of this seems like too much of a chore, a simpler alternative is to use a DataList or DataGrid. These controls will create a **Table** object for you and handle remembering its state.

Shock Number Three: Multi-Page Applications

Now that you know that pages only exist as objects while they are being processed, it may have occurred to you that creating multi-page applications is not quite the same. The way one page is called from another is completely different from calling a page in GUI development.

As a GUI developer, you might expect to create an instance of a **Page** class, set some properties, and activate it. However, Web applications just don't work that way—one page cannot have direct access to another. ASP developers are familiar with techniques for communicating with one page from another, but GUI developers will have some learning to do.

Transferring Control

There are two means of transferring control from one page to another:

- **Hyperlinks.** The HTML way to transfer control from one page to another is with a hyperlink. These can be declared using HTML <A> or using the HyperLink control. The advantage of hyperlinks is that they jump directly to the new page without doing a post-back to the current page.
- **Redirecting.** In some code that handles an event on the server, you can call the function Response.Redirect and pass in a URL as above. For example, this might typically be done after performing a database update.

Both techniques involve passing in a Universal Resource Locator (URL). These are typically simple relative references to another page in the same application. You can pass parameters from one page to another by embedding strings in the URL as described in the following section.

Transferring Information

Visual Basic users in particular may feel that transferring information from one page to anther is a bit of a throwback to the days of Visual Basic 3.0 and earlier—back when you often had to use global data to communicate between forms. This can be a bit of a pain, but the benefit is an application that can be used by thousands of people at one time instead of just one.

The following are ways to transfer information from one page to another:

URL parameters. In this way, strings are embedded in the URL. For example, to call a page titled WebForm2.aspx in the same directory and pass a single parameter "Foo" of value "Bar," you would use the URL *WebForm2.aspx?Foo=Bar*. The page being called would be able to access this parameter using the following code:

```
Dim Foo As String
Foo = CStr(Request.QueryString("Foo"))
```

Session state. This is the recommended way to remember complex or secure information. In some cases, even if you have only a single page application, you should consider using session state before using view state for security reasons. When writing code you can access the **Session** object, which is a collection of values that is associated with the user's browser session. Like the **State** object, the **Session** object is a collection of objects identified by strings. Like view state, it can store simple types as well as container types such as **Array**, **ArrayList**, **Hashtable**, and **DataSet**.

Application state. To store and read information that applies to all current users of your application, use the **Application** object, which has the same interface as session state and view state.

A Note About Security

It can be disturbingly easy to introduce security holes into your application simply because the Web is largely insecure. You should be aware of what is secure and what is not.

View state and URL parameters are both very insecure. Not only can someone see the values fairly easily, it's also possible for someone to change them and post them back. You should make sure no secure information is stored in these values, and that your data cannot get corrupted by someone changing them.

Session state and application state are secure. Because they exist on the server and are never exposed. There is no way for a hacker to modify these values unless you write code to allow it. Secure information should be stored in the session state or application state.

Validation is secure. It can be relied on because validation checks are always re-executed on the server, even if someone tries to hack around it on the client. Server validation is a security mechanism as well as a fallback to client validation.

Shock Number Four: Data Binding

The shock about data binding is that it no longer has to be a dirty word. In traditional GUI programming, data binding has often turned out to be a failure. One of the first big lessons that a Visual Basic programmer learns is that data binding is usually a lot more trouble than it is worth. You also will frequently run into problems building a real-world application using it. It has come to be used mostly for prototyping, reports, and data entry that requires no transactional control.

ASP+ data binding is more usable for building real business applications; ironically, this is because it has fewer features. There are two big differences between ASP+ data binding and traditional GUI data binding:

- **It is explicit.** You need to call the **DataBind** method of the **Page** class or the data-bound control for data binding to take place. Traditionally data binding gets called automatically, which makes it very difficult to control.
- **It is one-way.** In a typical business transaction, data binding would work fine for getting data out of a data base, but you generally want to do a lot of custom processing or call stored procedures or business objects to do the update. Because updating data sources automatically at the wrong time is usually what causes the problems, data binding will take information out of a data source; however, it leaves it to you to do the update. This gives you a lot more control while still being useful for reporting and prototyping.

Another benefit of the data binding model is that it also works with simple information in memory, such as an array of structures. In Visual Basic, data bound controls generally have two very distinct modes of operation depending on whether the data is supplied in memory or from a database. In the common language runtime, data binding works through low-level interfaces; therefore, it works the same with simple data structures as it does with data from a traditional database.

Conclusion

As you can see, Web development is a very different world from GUI development. This article was designed to help you avoid some of the most common pitfalls when switching between the two. Understanding the conceptual modal may help you work through most of the difficulties you will encounter.

A Platform for Web Services

In this article, Mary Kirtland of Microsoft Corporation presents an overview of the Web Services model for building applications. The article was published in January 2001 on MSDN Online. The main topics covered include the definition of Web Services; the generic architecture of a Web Service and how it relates to Microsoft Windows DNA and .NET; some requirements for a platform that provides support for building, deploying, or consuming Web Services; and the products and technologies provided by Microsoft to address those requirements.

Introduction

If you've been following the news about Microsoft® .NET, you'll know that Web Services play a major role in the .NET application architecture. In the .NET vision, an application is constructed using multiple Web Services that work together to provide data and services for the application. However, just because Web Services are usually discussed in the context of .NET, you should not assume that you must wait for the Microsoft .NET Framework or Microsoft® Visual Studio.NET to build, deploy, or consume Web Services. Web Services are a very general model for building applications and can be implemented for any operating system that supports communication over the Internet.

In this article, we will:

- Review the definition of Web Services.
- Define a generic architecture for Web Services and relate that architecture to Microsoft® Windows® DNA and .NET.
- Specify some requirements on a platform that provides good support for building, deploying, or consuming Web Services.
- Indicate the products and technologies provided by the Microsoft platform to address these requirements.

Web Services Defined

A Web Service is programmable application logic accessible using standard Internet protocols. Web Services combine the best aspects of component-based development and the Web. Like components, Web Services represent black-box functionality that can be reused without worrying about how the service is implemented. Unlike current component technologies, Web Services are not accessed via object-model-specific protocols, such as the distributed Component Object Model (DCOM), Remote Method Invocation (RMI), or Internet Inter-ORB Protocol (IIOP). Instead, Web Services are accessed via ubiquitous Web protocols and data formats, such as Hypertext Transfer Protocol (HTTP) and Extensible Markup Language (XML).

Furthermore, a Web Service interface is defined strictly in terms of the messages the Web Service accepts and generates. Consumers of the Web Service can be implemented on any platform in any programming language, as long as they can create and consume the messages defined for the Web Service interface.

There are a few key specifications and technologies you are likely to encounter when building or consuming Web Services. These specifications and technologies address five requirements for service-based development:

- A standard way to represent data
- A common, extensible, message format
- A common, extensible, service description language
- A way to discover services located on a particular Web site
- A way to discover service providers

XML is the obvious choice for a standard way to represent data. Most Web Service-related specifications use XML for data representation, as well as XML Schemas to describe data types.

The Simple Object Access Protocol (SOAP) defines a lightweight protocol for information exchange. Part of the SOAP specification defines a set of rules for how to use XML to represent data. Other parts of the SOAP specification define an extensible message format, conventions for representing remote procedure calls (RPCs) using the SOAP message format, and bindings to the HTTP protocol. (SOAP messages can be exchanged over other protocols, but the current specification only defines bindings for HTTP.) Microsoft anticipates that SOAP will be the standard message format for communicating with Web Services.

Given a Web Service, it would be nice to have a standard way to document what messages the Web Service accepts and generates—that is, to document the Web Service contract. A standard mechanism makes it easier for developers and developer tools to create and interpret contracts. The Web Services Description Language (WSDL) is an XML-based contract language jointly developed by Microsoft and IBM. We anticipate that WSDL will be widely supported by developer tools for creating Web Services.

Note Over the past year Microsoft and IBM have proposed several contract languages: Service Description Language (SDL), SOAP Contract Language (SCL), and Network Accessible Services Specification Language (NASSL). While these are all superceded by WSDL, some early development tools use these languages. You might need to translate the provided contract into the contract language your development tool understands in order to consume a Web Service.

Developers will also need some way to discover Web Services. The Discovery Protocol (Disco) specification defines a discovery document format (based on XML) and a protocol for retrieving the discovery document, enabling developers to discover services at a known URL. However, in many cases the developer will not know the URLs where services can be found. Universal Description, Discovery, and Integration (UDDI) specifies a mechanism for Web Service providers to advertise the existence of their Web Services and for Web Service consumers to locate Web Services of interest.

For more information about Web Services and these key specifications, see Web Services Essentials in the MSDN Library.

Web Services, Windows DNA, and .NET

Recall that the .NET vision imagines applications will be constructed from multiple Web Services that work together to provide data and services for the application. This is shown in Figure 1.

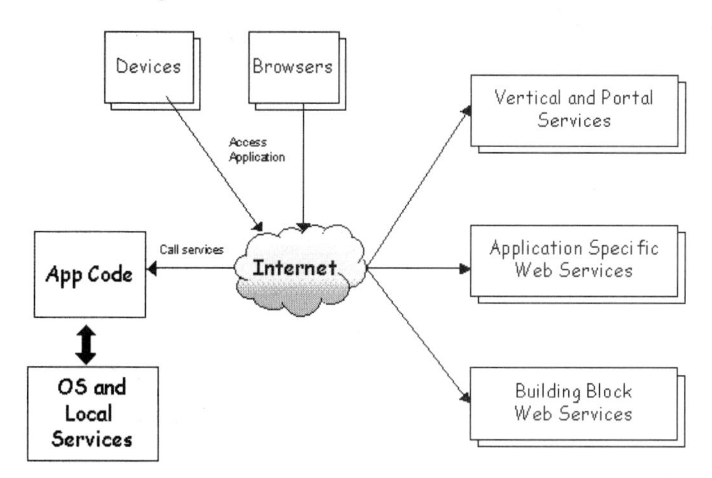

Figure 1. .NET application architecture

This diagram, as well as the definition of Web Services just provided, is concerned with the external appearance of the Web Services. After all, we've said that as long as a client application can create and consume the appropriate messages, it doesn't need to know anything about the internals of the Web Services it uses. Developers of Web Services will obviously care about the internal structure as well.

Figure 2 shows a generic architecture for a Web Service. The architecture is divided into five logical layers. Furthest from the client is the *data layer*, which stores information required by the Web Service. Above the data layer is the *data access layer*, which presents a logical view of the physical data to the business layer. The data access layer isolates business logic from changes to the underlying data stores and ensures the integrity of the data. The business layer implements the business logic of the Web Service. As in Figure 2, it is often subdivided into two parts: the *business façade* and the *business logic*. The business façade provides a simple interface that maps directly to operations exposed by the Web Service. The business façade uses services provided by the business logic layer. In a simple Web Service, all the business logic might be implemented by the business façade, which would interact directly with the data access layer. Client applications interact with the Web Service *listener*. The listener is responsible for receiving incoming messages containing requests for service, parsing the messages, and dispatching the request to the appropriate method on the business façade. If the service returns a response, the listener is also responsible for packaging the response from the business façade into a message and sending that back to the client. The listener also handles requests for contracts and other documents about the Web Service. If you think about it, the only part of the Web Service that knows it is part of a Web Service is the listener!

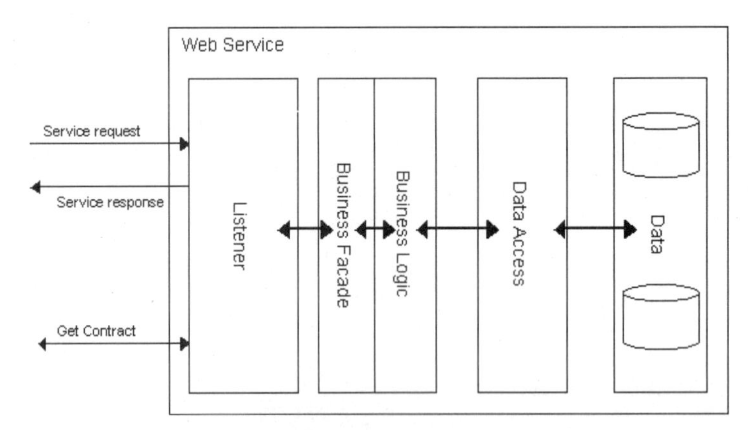

Figure 2. Generic Web Service architecture

This architecture is very similar to the *n*-tier application architecture defined by Windows DNA. As shown in Figure 3, the Web Service listener is equivalent to the presentation layer of a Windows DNA application. A common development scenario is likely to include exposing functionality of an existing Web application for programmatic access—that is, adding a Web Service to an existing application. As this figure shows, that could be as simple as implementing a Web Service listener that accesses the existing business facade.

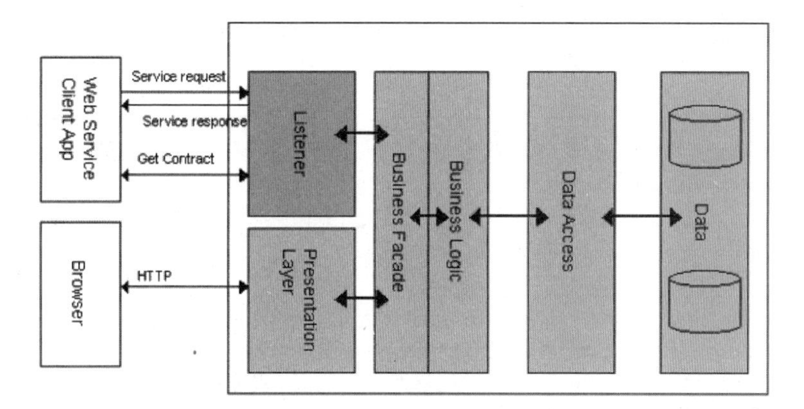

Figure 3. Relationship of Web Service architecture to Windows DNA architecture

In the Windows DNA architecture, we're used to thinking about implementing the data layer using databases and the business layer using COM components. But what if the data access layer gets its data from a Web Service instead of a database? Or the business façade calls a Web Service to do part of its work? Suddenly our application architecture looks a lot like Figure 1. In some respects, the .NET application architecture simply extends the Windows DNA application architecture across the Web.

Note The requirements and usage patterns for programmatic access will often be sufficiently different from the requirements and usage patterns of the existing Web application that additional work is required. These differences might impact all layers of the application architecture. For example, the physical data schema might not be designed to handle new kinds of queries exposed by a Web Service, or the volume of queries made by client applications. In addition, Web Services have extremely high reliability requirements. Unless your existing Web application is highly available, capable of dealing with unexpected input values, and so on, additional work might be needed to meet these new requirements.

Platform Requirements

Given the similarities between the Windows DNA architecture and the Web Services architecture, you should not be surprised to learn that developing Web Services is not all that different from developing Web applications, or that you can develop Web Services using today's Windows DNA technologies. However, there are some notable differences. In particular, in order to implement a Web Service listener, you'll probably need to understand SOAP messages and generate SOAP responses, provide a WSDL contract for your service and Disco file for your site, and advertise your service via UDDI. If you're consuming Web Services, you might need to use UDDI or Disco to locate services and service contracts, interpret a WSDL contract for the service, and generate appropriate SOAP messages and interpret SOAP responses.

In addition, because applications rely on Web Services, it is critical that these services are completely dependable. A Web Service should always be available. It must not make mistakes, lose requests, fault in the face of invalid requests, or corrupt persisted data. It should always be able to meet client demand with acceptable performance. In the rare event that a fault occurs, the Web Service should continue processing requests as best it can. In other words, a Web Service needs all the "abilities"—scalability, reliability, availability, and so on. If a Web Service is not dependable, application developers will not use it.

Note For more information on building scalable, reliable, and available Web applications, see the MSDN Online E-Commerce Resources page at http://msdn.microsoft.com/ecommerce/ (/ecommerce/default.asp). While the resources on these pages talk about Web applications, the techniques are applicable to Web Services as well.

Systems administrators for service providers will not permit Web Services to be deployed unless the Web Services are easy to deploy and manage. It should be possible to deploy a Web Service without using special tools, either locally or remotely. The deployment process should be easy to learn and easy to replicate. It should be easy to deploy a new version of a Web Service, either side by side with the existing version or by replacing the existing version. Management tools should make it easy to monitor and tune Web Service performance, both in isolation and in combination with other services, as demand varies. It must be possible to secure a Web Service so that only authorized consumers can use it. Perhaps most importantly, deploying one Web Service must not impact the availability or performance of any other Web Service—even if multiple Web Services share implementation components.

The requirements of Web Services consumers and system administrators impose a considerable burden on Web Service developers that's not specifically related to any functionality provided by the service. Web Service developers will want infrastructure and tools support that make it easier to implement secure, reliable, scalable, manageable, and highly available Web Services. Developers will also want infrastructure and tools to help them debug, profile, and trace execution of their code and the infrastructure services they are using. Ideally, you will not need to learn a new programming language in order to use this infrastructure and these tools. In fact, the more you can leverage your existing skills, components, applications, and data stores, the better.

Much of the difficulty in implementing scalable, highly available code is connected with properly managing resources—such as processes, threads, and shared state—when multiple concurrent requests are received by a service. Middleware that manages these resources and lets you write service logic as if a single client is accessing it can greatly improve the reliability, scalability, and availability of Web Services, as well as greatly simplify development of the Web Service.

In practical terms, the middleware provides a standard hosting environment for Web Service implementation code. The hosting environment is responsible for:

- Listening for incoming HTTP requests.
- Performing security authentication and authorization checks.
- Dispatching authorized requests to the correct service.
- Ensuring services are isolated from each other and the hosting environment—that is, a service has its own memory, services cannot block other services from executing, and service faults cannot cause other services or the hosting environment to fault.
- Automatically recovering from service, hosting environment, and system failures.
- Providing administrative facilities for deploying, monitoring, and controlling services.
- Managing resources such as processes, threads, and shared state on behalf of each service.

Of course, some Web Services will have non-standard requirements that the standard hosting environment does not support. Thus, the environment must be flexible enough that you can replace features that don't meet your needs.

APIs for constructing and parsing messages will also enhance your productivity. At a minimum, APIs must support reading and writing XML streams. Specific APIs for standards such as SOAP, WSDL, Disco, and UDDI will improve productivity as well as overall reliability by eliminating the need for you to write parsing and formatting logic. The APIs also reduce the need for you to learn every detail of the specifications.

If you are implementing Web Services using component technologies, additional productivity gains can be achieved if the system provides services to activate objects on demand and map messages to object method calls—essentially implementing the Web Service listener for you. Similarly, if you're consuming Web Services, you'll want tools that construct proxy objects hiding the details of formatting and sending a service request, then interpreting the response.

A Roadmap to the Microsoft Platform

Microsoft Windows 2000 provides the basic infrastructure required to implement Web applications and Web Services. Windows 2000 Internet Information Services (IIS) and Component Services (a.k.a. COM+) provide a hosting environment that meets most of the requirements just listed. Windows 2000 also provides APIs to help you implement all layers of a Web Service:

- COM for implementing the business façade, business logic, and data access layers
- ADO, OLE DB, and ODBC for implementing data access to a variety of data stores
- MSXML to help construct and consume XML messages in the Web Service listener
- Active Server Pages (ASP) or ISAPI for implementing the Web Service listener

To improve availability and scalability of your Web Service, you can use the Network Load Balancing (NLB) and Clustering services of Windows 2000 Advanced Server and Datacenter Server. Access to Web Services can be restricted using IPSec, HTTP Basic authentication, Digest authentication, Kerberos 5 authentication, NTLM authentication, or your own custom scheme. IPSec, SSL, and Windows cryptography services can be used to ensure data privacy.

.NET Enterprise Servers

Microsoft also supplies several server products you might find useful when implementing and deploying Web Services. The latest versions of these products, collectively known as the .NET Enterprise Servers, have been enhanced to support the Web and XML.

The .NET Enterprise Servers include:

- Application Center 2000, for deploying and managing your Web applications and Web Services.
- BizTalk™ Server 2000, for business process orchestration and document interchange. BizTalk Server contains extensive support for XML and SOAP-based messages, transmitted over a variety of protocols, including HTTP, SSL, and SMTP. Developers who are most interested in exposing business processes to their business partners will likely build solutions based on BizTalk Server that end up fitting the definition of a Web Service, rather than explicitly setting out to implement Web Services.
- Commerce Server 2000, an application platform for building e-commerce Web applications.
- Exchange Server 2000, for messaging and collaboration. Exchange 2000 includes the Microsoft Web Storage System, which provides hierarchical data storage of heterogeneous documents. XML is the native data format for many kinds of documents in the Web Storage System. Exchange is tightly integrated with IIS, to support SMTP, POP, and direct access to data via HTTP. Exchange provides a complete application platform for building collaborative workflow applications that work over the Web. As with BizTalk Server, developers who are most interested in building workflow applications will likely build solutions based on Exchange or Microsoft® SharePoint™ Portal Server that end up fitting the definition of a Web Service, rather than explicitly setting out to implement Web Services.
- Host Integration Server 2000, for accessing mainframe applications and data stores. Host Integration Server is the evolution of Microsoft SNA Server.
- Internet Security and Acceleration Server 2000, which provides firewall and Web caching services.

- Mobile Information Server 2001, for wireless access to enterprise data.
- SQL Server™ 2000, for relational data storage. SQL Server 2000 includes extensive support for XML. Relational data can be queried and modified as XML, eliminating the need to handcraft formatting logic in your applications. You can also provide direct access to SQL Server data stores and OLAP cubes via HTTP, using the SQL Server XML services. If your Web Service simply handles queries for data without a great deal of business logic and you don't need to provide a SOAP-based interface, you might consider simply using SQL Server XML as the Web Service listener.

Today's Tools for SOAP

Note that, with the exception of BizTalk Server 2000, these technologies and products do not support SOAP, WSDL, Disco, or UDDI. Developers creating SOAP-based Web Services with today's technologies have three basic choices:

- Roll-your-own, using MSXML, ASP, or ISAPI, etc. The downside to this, of course, is that you need to implement and test everything yourself—and figure out how to comply with the relevant specifications!
- Use the SOAP Toolkit for Visual Studio 6.0 to build a Web Service listener that connects to a business façade implemented using COM. (The SOAP Toolkit can be used if the business façade is not implemented as a COM component, but you cannot leverage the wizard that generates the listener as easily.) Note that the SOAP Toolkit is a sample provide by MSDN. The Toolkit understands SOAP over HTTP and SSL, but does not help you create Disco documents or UDDI registrations. It supports an older contract language called SDL, rather than WSDL.
- Use the Microsoft Soap Toolkit version 2 to build a Web Service listener that connects to a business façade implemented using COM. The Microsoft Soap Toolkit version 2 is scheduled to for publication on MSDN Online in the first quarter of 2001. Version 2 supports SOAP over HTTP, and can be used to create a WSDL file describing your service. You will still need to create Disco documents and UDDI registrations manually.

Both versions of the SOAP Toolkit provide tools to help developers consume Web Services as if they were COM components. The SOAP Toolkit provides a COM component called the Remote Object Proxy Engine (ROPE) that can be used by client applications. ROPE uses an SDL file to dynamically create Automation methods you can call on a proxy object. If you want to use a Web Service that doesn't supply an SDL file, you will need to create one. Version 2 of the SOAP Toolkit provides similar functionality, based on WSDL files.

Moving Forward with .NET

The .NET Framework is Microsoft's next-generation platform for building Web applications and Web Services. It is built from the ground up to meet the needs of Web Services developers and consumers, with pervasive support for Web standards such as XML and SOAP. Some of the key features of the .NET Framework for Web Services developers include:

- *A common language runtime* that manages the needs of running code written in any programming language and eliminates the need to implement special interfaces such as **IUnknown** and **IDispatch**. Developers simply implement classes in their chosen programming language. Classes are completely self-describing, so there's no need for separate type libraries or IDL files.
- *Interoperability with existing COM components.* Existing COM components look like managed classes to managed applications; managed classes look like COM components to unmanaged applications.
- *An improved application deployment model,* which lets you specify exactly what versions of dependent DLLs to use. Application configuration information can be specified in text files, simplifying administration of applications. Many applications can be deployed by simply copying files on to the target machine (sometimes called "Xcopy Deployment").
- *Integrated, pervasive security services* to ensure that unauthorized users cannot access code or perform unauthorized actions.
- *ADO.NET,* which provides classes to access XML documents and relational data stores. As the name implies, ADO.NET is the evolution of Microsoft ActiveX® Data Objects (ADO).
- *Lightweight application isolation* based on application domains. An application domain represents an isolation boundary. An isolated application can be independently stopped and debugged, cannot access code or resources of other applications, can fault without causing other applications to fail, and has a baseline set of authorization checks that can be performed before the application is launched. Multiple application domains can run within the same process.
- *A robust HTTP runtime* for processing HTTP requests, engineered to automatically recover as best it can from access violations, memory leaks, deadlocks, and so on. Web applications and Web Services run in application domains, so a fault in one application domain doesn't bring down other application domains or the hosting environment. Application domains are launched on demand; if a fault stops an application domain, the next incoming request simply launches a new one. The runtime also supports preemptive cycling of applications to improve overall system stability in the face of applications that leak resources. Application DLLs are never locked, so new versions can be deployed without shutting down the application or Web server—when a new DLL is detected, a new application domain is launched to handle new requests and any existing application domains are shut down when they have no outstanding requests.

- *ASP.NET*, which provides a low-level programming model equivalent to ISAPI (but easier to implement), along with high-level programming models for building Web applications (known as Web Forms) and Web Services. ASP.NET supports basic, digest, and NTLM authentication, as well as Microsoft Passport authentication and custom cookie-based authentication for applications that use a private account database for authenticating users.
- *.NET Remoting* for activating objects and making method calls across context, application domain, process, or machine boundaries. For cross-machine calls, .NET Remoting supports both a DCOM-like binary wire protocol over TCP/IP and the SOAP wire protocol over HTTP or SMTP. The architecture is extensible, so that additional wire protocols and transports can be supported.

ASP.NET Web Services are the preferred technology for implementing Web Services based on the .NET Framework. ASP.NET Web Services support service requests using SOAP over HTTP, as well as HTTP **GET** or **POST**. ASP.NET Web Services automatically generate WSDL and Disco files for your Web Services. You can use ASP.NET Web Services to implement a Web Service listener that accesses a business façade implemented as a COM component or managed class. The .NET Framework SDK also provides tools to generate proxy classes that client applications can use to access Web Services.

Note that ASP.NET Web Services, as with the other tools we have discussed, do not expose the server-side types to client applications. The implementation is completely hidden inside the Web Service. All the tools discussed assume a stateless programming model as well—that is, each incoming request is handled independently. The only state maintained between requests is anything persisted in data stores.

If you need a more tightly coupled, object-based programming model between client and server, you'll want to use .NET Remoting. .NET Remoting provides remote access to server-side objects with full type fidelity. Clients can obtain references to server-side objects and control the lifetime of those objects. If you use these object lifetime services, however, client applications will need to be implemented using .NET Remoting as well.

In addition to the features provided by the .NET Framework, Microsoft Visual Studio.NET provides additional tools to help you build, deploy, and consume Web Services. For example, the IDE supports UDDI and Disco for locating Web Services, and understands how to generate client-side proxies from WSDL files. Visual Studio.NET also includes ATL Server, which C++ developers using ATL can use to construct Web Service listeners that connect to a business façade implemented as a C++ class. ATL Server supports SOAP over HTTP and will automatically generate WSDL files for your Web Services. It also provides tools to generate C++ proxy classes that client applications can use to access Web Services.

As you can see, Microsoft provides a number of tools and technologies that will help you build, deploy, and consume Web Services. The centerspread in the January/February 2001 issue of *MSDN News* (see http://msdn.microsoft.com/voices/news/roadmap.asp) provides a handy roadmap to help you sort through the options discussed in this article, as well as pointers to more information about each product. Note that the centerspread does not try to list every option for implementing a Web Service. Instead, it attempts to recommend good options for different development scenarios, given the current capabilities of Microsoft products.

Introducing ADO+: Data Access Services for the Microsoft .NET Framework

In this article, Omri Gazitt, Group Program Manager on the Microsoft WebData team, discusses ActiveX Data Objects (ADO+)—the .NET class framework for data access. This article was published in the November 2000 issue of MSDN Magazine. Topics discussed include the design motivations behind ADO+; the various classes in the two layers that make up the ADO+ framework—the connected Managed Providers and the disconnected DataSet; key aspects of DataSets, including populating data stores, relationships, filtering, searching, and data views; and the integration of ADO+ with the .NET XML framework.

Microsoft has recently introduced a new platform for developing applications—the .NET Framework. At the Professional Developer's Conference 2000, Microsoft unveiled many new technologies that make up the new framework—the Common Language Runtime (CLR), Active Server Pages+ (ASP+), Web Forms and Win Forms programming environments, and the many class libraries that comprise the Class Framework.

The Microsoft .NET Framework (see Figure 1) offers developers many advantages over the traditional COM environment, including automatic object lifetime management, language-neutral class libraries, and cross-language inheritance, exception handling, and debugging.

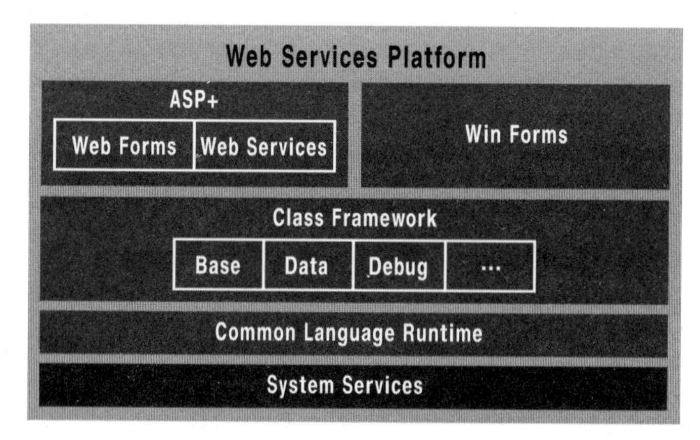

Figure 1. Microsoft .NET Framework

ActiveX® Data Objects (ADO+) is the new set of classes that expose data access services to the .NET programmer. It is an integral part of the Class Framework, which contains the entire library of classes that Microsoft provides with .NET, including the base classes for the primitive system types, I/O, network, data, and XML. This article offers a glimpse into the design motivations behind ADO+ and provides an introduction to the two layers of the ADO+ object model—Managed Providers and DataSets. Following that, this article will discuss the integration of ADO+ with the XML framework, and will conclude with a description of how the Visual Studio® .NET data designers provide design-time support for the ADO+ classes.

Why Another Data Access API?

Microsoft is known for releasing new data access APIs quite frequently, often to the chagrin of its development community. Why then is there yet another in this succession? The answer lies in the evolving face of application development. Most new applications are loosely coupled based on the Web application model, and more and more of these applications use XML to encode data on the wire. Web applications use HTTP as the fabric for communication between tiers, and therefore must explicitly handle maintaining state between requests. This new model is very different from the connected, tightly coupled style of programming that characterized the client/server era, where a connection was held open for the duration of the program's lifetime and no special handling of state was required.

The existing data access infrastructure, including ADO and OLE DB, was designed for a tightly coupled, connected environment. The Microsoft Data Access Component (MDAC) stack of services evolved primarily to keep up with the emerging Internet era. Remote Data Services (RDS) introduced the disconnected recordset to enable developers to continue to use the familiar ADO programming model in Web scenarios. HTTP support was added to RDS so that client-side script could easily call middle-tier business logic and retrieve a recordset. ADO was also given the ability to load and save disconnected recordsets into and out of a specific XML schema. However, much of the connected face of the programming model still shows through, and developers are faced with an increased learning curve in trying to figure out the right aspects of the model to use in a given scenario.

Developers were also finding it difficult to reconcile the ADO data model, which is primarily relational, with the new world of XML where the data model is heterogeneous and hierarchical. Since XML comes with its own object model (XMLDOM), and a different set of services (XSL/T, X-Path, W3C Schemas), developers have to make a binary choice about which stack they use—MDAC or MSXML—when what they really want is to use both technologies in a complementary fashion.

None of these challenges by themselves would have led Microsoft to redesign its flagship data access programming model, and indeed the introduction of ADO+ in no way makes ADO obsolete, as you will see later in this article. However, when Microsoft first envisioned the .NET Framework, it was clear that an entirely new programming model for data access was needed. The strength of the .NET Framework is in its uniformity—all components share a common type system, design patterns, and naming conventions. Additionally, reproducing ADO for the .NET Framework was not only contrary to the design principles of the framework, it was also not feasible. ADO is a mature technology, complete with its own idiosyncrasies and nuances. In fact, many developers have grown to rely on some behaviors that were originally just bugs in ADO! Reproducing the programming model with any degree of fidelity would have been a nearly insurmountable task.

The approach that Microsoft took was two-pronged. First, ADO has been made available to the .NET programmer through the .NET COM interoperability services, so developers can continue to rely on the same object model with all of its existing behavior, since they are invoking the same code under the covers. Second, some new classes have been introduced that are native to the .NET Framework—these classes are now called ADO+. This article concentrates on this new class framework, but first let's take a look at the design goals behind ADO+.

Evolution, Not Revolution

Microsoft's design for ADO+ needed to solve many of the problems inherent in the current data access services model. At the same time, the programming model needed to stay as similar as possible to ADO, so developers didn't have to learn yet another brand new data access technology. Microsoft also wanted to make the ADO+ object model feel like an intrinsic part of the overall class framework without making things difficult for the ADO programmer. ADO+ strikes a nice balance between the two.

Another key goal for ADO+ was to implement improvements in the ADO model so that ADO+ would have first-class support for the disconnected, *n*-tier programming environment for which most new applications are written. As a result, the concept of the disconnected recordset has been greatly enhanced and elevated to become the focal point in the programming model.

XML support was also a key design goal. XML and data access are intimately tied—XML is all about encoding data, and data access is increasingly becoming all about XML. The .NET Framework does not just support Web standards—it is built entirely on top of them. XML support is built into ADO+ at a very fundamental level. Plus, the XML class framework in .NET and ADO+ are really part of the same architecture—they integrate at many different levels. You no longer have to choose between the data access set of services and their XML counterparts—the ability to cross over from one to the other is inherent in the design of both.

The ADO+ Object Mode

The ADO+ object model is broadly divided into two levels: the connected layer, which consists of the classes that comprise the Managed Provider, and the disconnected layer, which is rooted in the DataSet. Let's look at the connected layer first, since this is what ADO programmers will already feel familiar with. Then I'll take a close look at the DataSet.

Managed Providers

Managed Providers are a core part of the ADO+ programming model. A Managed Provider loosely maps to the concept of an OLE DB provider, but the object model looks a lot more like ADO. Here you can see one of the advantages of the .NET Framework—the ability to write language-neutral components that can be called from C++ and Visual Basic®.This means that there is no longer a dichotomy of the low-level, high-performance COM components, and the slower automation layers that can be called from Visual Basic. In the .NET Framework, the OLE DB and ADO layers could indeed be merged into one layer that features high performance, and at the same time is callable from any language.

A Managed Provider consists of Connection, Command, DataReader, and DataSetCommand classes (see Figure 2). The first two should feel familiar to an ADO programmer; they are used to open a connection to a data source and execute a command against it, respectively. The DataReader loosely corresponds to a forward-only, read-only recordset. It is a highly optimized, nonbuffering, firehose-style interface for getting the results of a query executed against the data source. Finally, the DataSetCommand provides the bridge between the Managed Provider and the DataSet.

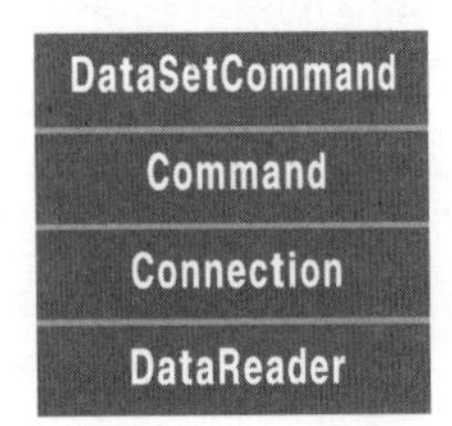

Figure 2. Managed Provider

The code in the following example shows how to open a connection to a database, execute a command against it, and consume the results.

Visual Basic

```
Imports System.Data
Imports System.Data.ADO
...
Dim myReader as ADODataReader = nothing
Dim myConnection as new ADOConnection( "Provider=SQLOLEDB.1;Integrated
Security=SSPI;Persist Security Info=False; Initial Catalog=Northwind;Data
Source=localhost")
  Dim myCommand as new ADOCommand("Select * from authors", myConnection)

  Try
    MyConnection.Open()
    MyCommand.Execute(myReader)

    While (myReader.Read)
      Console.WriteLine("author name: {0}", myReader("au_fname"))
    End while

  Catch myException as Exception
    MessageBox.Show(myException.ToString())
  Finally
    If myConnection.State = Data.DBObjectState.Open then
      MyConnection.Close()
    End if
    If not myReader is nothing then
      MyReader = nothing
    End if
  End Try
```

C#

```
using System.Data;
using System.Data.ADO;
...
ADOConnection myConnection = new ADOConnection("Provider=SQLOLEDB.1;Integrated
Security=SSPI;Persist Security Info=False; Initial Catalog=Northwind;Data
Source=localhost");
ADOCommand myCommand = new ADOCommand("Select * from authors", _
                                      myConnection);
ADODataReader myReader = null;
```

(continued)

(continued)

```
try
{
  myConnection.Open();
  myCommand.Execute(out myReader);
  if (myReader != null)
    while (myReader.Read())
      Console.WriteLine("author name: {0}", myReader["au_fname"]);
}
catch (Exception e)
{
  MessageBox.Show(e.ToString());
}
finally
{
  if (myConnection.State == DBObjectState.Open)
    myConnection.Close();
  if (null != myReader)
    myReader = null;
}
```

Let's walk through this code. First, you will note the "Imports" and "using" directives for Visual Basic and C#, respectively. Specifying these directives enables use of the classes in the System.Data and System.Data.ADO namespaces without having to fully qualify their names (as in System.Data. ADO.ADOConnection). Next, a connection is allocated and passed the connect string in the constructor. Then, a command is allocated and passed the command string and associated connection in its constructor. Finally, a DataReader is declared. Inside the try-catch-finally block, the code opens the connection, executes the command, and returns a DataReader as an output parameter. If the DataReader returns a non-null value, the result set is read record-by-record using the DataReader.Read method, displaying the contents of the author name field. The only syntax that might look unfamiliar is the while loop on the DataReader. In Visual Basic 6.0, the code would look like the following:

```
Set myRS = myCommand.Execute
Do While (Not myRS.EOF)
  Debug.Output myRS("au_fname")
  MyRS.MoveNext
Loop
```

The equivalent code in Visual Basic .NET now looks like this:

```
myDR = myCommand.Execute
While (myDR.Read)
  Debug.Output myDR("au_fname")
End While
```

The main difference here is that the DataReader is not positioned on the first row by default—you have to call the Read method explicitly to get to the first record. One of the reasons for this design choice is that many people forget to put the MoveNext call at the end of their loop—so the new pattern for using the DataReader is less error-prone.

Finally, note that the classes used in this example are all prefixed with "ADO" because this example uses the ADO Managed Provider. This Managed Provider sits on top of OLE DB, and can be used to communicate with any data source for which an OLE DB provider exists. The .NET Framework also ships with a Managed Provider that's built specifically for SQL Server™—the SQL Managed Provider. Replace all occurrences of "ADO" with "SQL" in the previous example, and you will be using the SQL Managed Provider. The SQL Managed Provider sits directly on top of TDS (the SQL Server wire format), and therefore provides significantly better performance against SQL Server than you would get going through the ADO Managed Provider and the SQL Server OLE DB provider (SQLOLEDB).

So now that there are Managed Providers, is OLE DB going away? Hardly. OLE DB is a specification that exposes data stores in a very rich way. It is a set of interfaces that covers all the features of all of the different types of data stores out there—in other words, a superset of all the store APIs. A key design goal was the ability to replace any existing store's proprietary API with OLE DB. By contrast, Managed Providers have taken the opposite approach: the lowest common set of functionality is exposed to the developer. The result is that interacting with a Managed Provider is extremely easy, and it is quite easy to create one as well; however, the functionality that it exposes is minimal.

So who should write a Managed Provider? In the past, Microsoft recommended writing an OLE DB provider (or OLE DB Simple Provider) for any type of data that needed to be exposed to an application. These days, however, if it's only data that needs to be exposed, Microsoft recommends that it simply be encoded as XML—so it can plug directly into the rich set of XML services that Microsoft provides. If a true store (with rich functionality) is to be exposed, create an OLE DB provider for it. This enables the store to plug into both the .NET Framework using the ADO Managed Provider, and the many rich OLE DB consumers available (such as Microsoft Excel, Microsoft Access, and the SQL Server distributed query processor, replication engine, and Data Transformation Service). Finally, if a data store vendor has a proprietary wire format, creating a Managed Provider will result in some significant performance benefits. Since there will invariably be many people who will want to write one, a Managed Provider SDK is scheduled to ship in a future .NET beta.

The DataSet

Now let's look at the disconnected layer, the DataSet. The simplest way to describe the DataSet is as a local buffer of tables, or a collection of disconnected recordsets. One important difference between a DataSet and a collection of disconnected recordsets is that the DataSet keeps track of the relationships between the tables it contains—it is in many ways an in-memory relational store. The DataSet also exposes a rich programming model that is only possible because all data is known to be stored in a local cache.

This is in contrast, the disconnected recordset, which only supports the standard MoveFirst, MoveNext, MovePrevious, MoveLast methods of the connected recordset. This difference is the key philosophical departure from ADO: instead of trying to roll many different concepts (forward-only, client, and server cursors) into one object, and thereby only being able to expose their lowest common denominator, ADO+ separates them. By making the DataSet a first-class citizen, all the underlying richness of the client cache can be exposed.

As shown in Figure 3, the DataSet object model consists of Tables, Columns, Relations, Constraints, and Rows. The first four of these together comprise the relational schema of the DataSet, while Rows are where the actual data is stored.

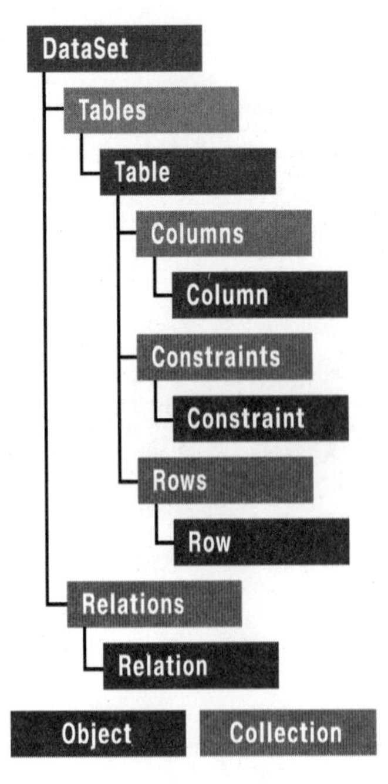

Figure 3. DataSet Object Model

A DataSet contains a collection of DataTables (the Tables collection). A DataTable represents one table of in-memory data. It contains a collection of columns (the Columns collection) that represents the table's schema. A DataTable also contains a collection of rows (the Rows collection), representing the data held by the table. It remembers the original state along with current state, tracking the kinds of changes that have occurred. The following example shows how a DataTable's schema and data can be created programmatically.

Visual Basic

```
Dim tb as DataTable
Dim col as DataColumn
Dim pkColArray(1) as DataColumn
Dim i as integer
Dim workRow as DataRow
tb = new DataTable("Customers")

col = new DataColumn("CustomerID", System.Type.GetType("System.Int32"))
tb.Columns.Add(col)
col.AllowNull = false
col.Unique = true

col = tb.Columns.Add("CustomerName", System.Type.GetType("System.String"))
col = tb.Columns.Add("Purchases", System.Type.GetType("System.Double"))

col = tb.Columns.Add("Rebates")
col.DataType = System.Type.GetType("System.Currency")
col.Expression = "Purchases * .1"

pkColArray(0) = tb.Columns("CustomerID")
tb.PrimaryKey = pkColArray

For i = 0 to 9
  workRow = tb.NewRow()
  workRow("CustomerID") = i
  workRow("CustomerName") = "CustName" & i.ToString()
  tb.Rows.Add(workRow)
Next
```

C#

```
DataColumn col = null;
DataTable tb = new DataTable("Customers");

col = new DataColumn("CustomerID", typeof(System.Int32));
tb.Columns.Add(col);
col.AllowNull = false;
col.Unique = true;

col = tb.Columns.Add("CustomerName", typeof(System.String));
col = tb.Columns.Add("Purchases", typeof(System.Double));

col = tb.Columns.Add("Rebates");
col.DataType = typeof(System.Currency);
col.Expression = "Purchases * .1";

tb.PrimaryKey = new DataColumn[] {tb.Columns["CustomerID"]};

DataRow workRow = null;
for (int i = 0; i <= 9; i++)
{
  workRow = tb.NewRow();
  workRow[0] = i;
  workRow[1] = "CustName" + i.ToString();
  tb.Rows.Add(workRow);
}
```

This example creates a new DataTable with the name Customers, then adds columns to the DataTable, demonstrating a couple of different ways to do so. In all cases, the columns are added to the DataTable using the Add method on the Columns collection, and the column is assigned a name and a datatype. The CustomerID column is set as a unique, non-nullable column (this will be the primary key of the table), while the Rebates column is given an expression that is driven off of the Purchases column, demonstrating the DataSet expression language capabilities. Next, the primary key of the table is created from a combination of any number of columns, represented as an array of DataColumns. In this example, the primary key is just the CustomerID column. Finally, data is added to the table by calling the NewRow method on the DataTable and storing the column values in each DataRow. Note that the Visual Basic code indexes into the DataRow using the column name, while the C# code indexes using the column ordinal. Of course both forms are valid for any language.

Now let's see how to load a DataSet using a DataSetCommand, how table relationships allow for navigation and data retrieval between tables, how the Select method provides support for filtering and searching, and finally how the DataSet supports setting constraints on data.

Populating DataSets with DataSetCommands

I've shown how to load schema and data into the DataSet using the object model directly. A DataSet can also be populated using the DataSetCommand object of a Managed Provider, or by loading XML in directly. What is important to remember is that regardless of how it is loaded, the DataSet never has any knowledge of the source of the data it contains. It keeps track of any changes that are made via the object model, and exposes these changes programmatically so that a DataSetCommand can obtain them at any time and update the data source in an optimistic fashion. The following example shows how to load the DataSet using a DataSetCommand.

Visual Basic

```
Dim myDS as DataSet
Dim myDSCommand as SQLDataSetCommand
Dim myCustomer as DataRow

myDS = new DataSet
myDSCommand = new SQLDataSetCommand("Select * from customers", _
  "server=localhost;uid=sa;pwd=;database=northwind")
myDSCommand.FillDataSet(myDS, "Customers")

For Each myCustomer in myDS.Tables(0).Rows
  Console.WriteLine(myCustomer("CustomerID").ToString())
Next
```

C#

```
DataSet myDS = new DataSet();
SQLDataSetCommand myDSCommand = new SQLDataSetCommand("select * from \
  customers", "server=localhost;uid=sa;pwd=;database=northwind");
myDSCommand.FillDataSet(myDS, "Customers");

foreach (DataRow myCustomer in myDS.Tables[0].Rows)
  Console.WriteLine(myCustomer["CustomerID"].ToString());
```

In this example, a DataSetCommand is created, and a connection string and SQL statement are passed to the constructor. Under the covers, the DataSetCommand creates a Connection object, which it assigns to its ActiveConnection property, and a Command object, which is assigned to the SelectCommand property. Of course, this can be done by coding explicitly to the Connection and Command objects as well. The DataSetCommand's FillData Set method is then called, passing in a DataSet. Note that the DataSetCommand can create both the schema and the data inside of the DataSet. If a DataTable called Customers already existed in the DataSet, the data would simply be added to that table (and the schema of the table augmented as necessary).

Also note that the connection that was created is closed after the DataSetCommand finishes loading the DataSet. This is in agreement with the disconnected nature of the operation—the connection is only open long enough for the command to be executed and the data loaded into the DataSet.

In addition to the SelectCommand property, the DataSetCommand also has InsertCommand, UpdateCommand, and DeleteCommand properties. These properties are used when the DataSetCommand's Update method is called. At that point, the DataSetCommand opens the connection and fires off the appropriate insert/update/delete commands against the data source, corresponding to the changes that were made to data in the DataSet.

Table Relationships in DataSets

As mentioned earlier, a DataSet can hold multiple tables and can store relationships between them. The advantage in telling a DataSet about the relationships among the tables it contains is that its programming model allows direct navigation between the related tables.

But how can you create a relationship between two tables? The following example presumes that two DataTable objects exist in the DataSet. Both tables have a column named CustomerID which serves as the link between the two tables. The example adds a single DataRelation to the DataSet object's Relations collection. The first argument (CustOrders) specifies the name of the relation. The second and third arguments are the DataColumn objects that link the two tables (one as a primary key, one as a foreign key).

```
'in Visual Basic
  Dim ds As DataSet = New DataSet("CustomerOrders")
  ds.Relations.Add("CustOrders",
                    ds.Tables("Customers").Columns("CustomerID"), _
                    ds.Tables("Orders").Columns("CustomerID"))

// in C#
  DataSet ds = new DataSet("CustomerOrders");
  ds.Relations.Add("CustOrders",
                    ds.Tables["Customers"].Columns["CustomerID"],
                    ds.Tables["Orders"].Columns["CustomerID"]);
```

So what can you do now that you have a relationship in place? A primary function of the DataRelation is to allow navigation from one table to another within the DataSet. In practice, this allows you to retrieve all of the related DataRow objects in one table when given a single DataRow from a related table. For example, if you have a DataRow from the Customers table, you can retrieve all of the orders for a particular customer from the Orders table. The code in the following example returns an array of DataRow objects (orders) from one table using the DataRelation and the single DataRow from another (customers).

Visual Basic

```
Dim cust As DataRow = ds.Tables("Customers").Rows(0)
Dim orders() As DataRow = cust.GetChildRows(ds.Relations("CustomerOrders")
Console.WriteLine("Total Child records for CustOrders Relationship = " & _
  "orders.Length.ToString)
```

C#

```
DataRow cust = ds.Tables["Customers"].Rows[0];
DataRow[] orders = cust.GetChildRows(ds.Relations["CustomerOrders"]);
Console.WriteLine("Total Child records for CustOrders Relationship = " +
orders.Length.ToString());
```

Additional Relational Capabilities

The DataSet has a Select method that can be used to return an array of DataRows that matches the filter criteria. The following example returns DataRows only for CustomerID's that begin with the letter A:

```
'in Visual Basic
  Dim CurrRows() As DataRow = workTable.Select("CustomerID like 'A%'")

// in C#
  DataRow[] CurrRows = workTable.Select("CustomerID like 'A%'");
```

Much like a relational database, the DataSet also provides the ability to set constraints on the values of a column. Both unique constraints and cascading constraints are supported. If you need to make updates that would violate integrity as determined by constraints, the BeginEdit and EndEdit methods can be used to defer constraint validation until EndEdit is called.

The DataSet also contains a mechanism to accept or reject changes that are made to it in batch. As mentioned before, a DataSet keeps track of all the changes made to it. Every row really has three values that are stored for each column: original, current, and proposed values. Original values represent the original data that came from the source and can be used for optimistic conflict resolution; current values are the working copy of the data; and proposed values are the intermediate column values that are set between BeginEdit and EndEdit calls. When the user calls AcceptChanges, the current values become the original values; RejectChanges reverts the current values back to the original ones.

Finally, the DataSet supports a rich event model. A developer can register delegates for ColumnChange, RowChanged, RowChanging, RowDeleting, and RowDeleted on a DataTable, and PropertyChange, MergeFailed, RemoveTable, and RemoveRelation on a DataSet. The RowChanging and RowDeleting events allow changes to be suppressed, while the RowChanged and RowDeleted events are fired after the change has already been made.

Server Cursors

As I described earlier, ADO's recordset was really a conflation of three different APIs—the interface for a forward-only stream of data, the API for a client-side cache (the OLE DB cursor engine), and an abstraction for exposing updateable, scrollable cursors. The first two map to the ADO+ DataReader and DataSet classes, respectively. So what happened to server cursors? ADO+ currently does not have intrinsic support for a general-purpose server cursor object. The key reason for this is that for this kind of functionality, data sources tend to differ in their implementation enough that exposing a single abstraction that hides the details from the user becomes difficult.

Since most applications require only the first two abstractions anyway, ADO+ relies on ADO for server cursor support, at least for the current beta of Visual Studio.NET. ADO is readily accessible from the .NET Framework through the COM Interop services of the CLR. The TLBIMP program, shipped with the SDK, can be used to import a COM type library and emit metadata that can be consumed by the CLR. Therefore, for developers who really want ADO semantics, or ones who rely heavily on positioned updates and connected scrollable cursors, using ADO through the Interop layer is the right solution.

XML Integration

One of the most important design goals for ADO+ was powerful XML support. Microsoft designed ADO+ hand-in-hand with the .NET XML Framework—both are components of a single architecture.

The convergence of ADO+ with the XML Framework happens in the DataSet. For starters, the DataSet has methods that can both read and write XML. For reading XML in, the XML Framework parser is used, either explicitly (if an XmlReader is passed into the ReadXml method) or implicitly (via overloads that take other parameters, such as a filename). For writing XML out, the XML Framework well-formed writer (XmlWriter) is employed. Note that regardless of where the data originated, the DataSet can save out its contents (both schema and data) as XML. The schema is encoded as an internal W3C Schema section, commonly known as XSD, and the data is encoded as XML that conforms to that schema.

Because the DataSet's native serialization format is XML, it is an excellent medium for moving data between tiers in a disconnected fashion just like the disconnected recordset. Indeed, .NET Web Services make heavy use of DataSets to transport data in the context of a schema between tiers of an application.

Just like populating the DataSet via its object model or through Managed Providers, loading the DataSet with XML is a two-stage process. First, the schema is created, and then the data is loaded. If the XML document comes with a schema, that schema is used to create the relational structure of the DataSet. If not, the DataSet can infer schema from the containment relationships within the document—generally speaking, elements that are not scalar-valued are mapped to tables, whereas attributes and scalar-valued elements are mapped to columns. The process of inferring schema is useful when first constructing an application that has to consume XML that comes with no schema. But for production applications, it is highly desirable to take the inferred schema, modify it as appropriate, and load that schema in before the actual data is loaded. That way, the process of loading the document is deterministic, so you don't have to worry about what a slight change in the incoming document will do to the inference heuristics.

Whatever the means for setting the DataSet's schema, when it comes time to load XML into the DataSet the following rules are used:

- Elements with a certain name are mapped into the DataSet table of the same name.
- Attributes and scalar-valued subelements are mapped into columns of that table.
- The schema of the table is expanded as appropriate if the columns aren't already in the DataSet, or if the DataSet doesn't already contain a table by the same name.

The following example shows how to load XML into the DataSet.

Visual Basic

```
Dim r As StreamReader = New StreamReader("foo.xml")
Dim ds as DataSet = New DataSet
ds.ReadXml(r)
```

C#

```
StreamReader r = new StreamReader("foo.xml");
DataSet ds = new DataSet();
ds.ReadXml(r);
```

When loading an XML schema into the DataSet, a table is created for each complex type in the schema, and containment is expressed using primary key/foreign key relationships. The key columns are automatically injected into the schema, and a DataRelation is added for each pair of related tables. Therefore, when loading data that resides in multiple tables from SQL Server 2000 or any other database that supports XML, it is in some ways more convenient to use the XML loading facilities rather than the DataSetCommand. The former enables loading all the data in one step, whereas the latter requires a DataSetCommand per table, and also entails setting up the relationships between the tables manually.

But some data has both a hierarchical structure and a partial relational structure, and you want to be able to round-trip the data and feed it to various applications. How does this work? The XmlDataDocument, a subclass of the XmlDocument, makes this possible.

The XmlDataDocument

The process of reading the XML into the DataSet is known as shredding. This term originates from the fact that the XML is mapped into tables, and some of the inherent hierarchical structure and document characteristics (such as ordering and whitespace) are lost. This is appropriate for many applications, since the XML that the applications have to read originates from highly structured sources (a relational database such as SQL Server 2000 that emits XML, for example)—so there is no loss of important information from the shredding process. However, many applications will expect to read documents that have only partial relational content.

A good example is a purchase order—a hierarchical document with a relational subset (line items). Ideally, you could still treat this kind of semi-structured data as a document, but be able to view the relational content using a relational API (such as the DataSet). Moreover, after the relational content is modified (using controls bound to that DataSet, for instance), saving that document out should retain all of its original structure and fidelity. The only difference from the original document should be the new values for the nodes that correspond to the rows that were changed. This enables round-tripping business documents through the relational infrastructure, a scenario that will become increasingly important in the emerging B2B world.

The XmlDataDocument provides that same functionality in ADO+. This object is a subclass of the XmlDocument (the .NET version of the W3C-DOM), so it is a full-fidelity representation of the XML document. But the XmlDataDocument is a special kind of DOM—it can be loaded with schema mappings, and that schema is used at load-time to determine how to map the document relationally. When the document is loaded, the relational subset can be obtained using the DataSet property on the XmlDataDocument (see the following example).

Visual Basic

```
imports System.NewXml
...
Dim r As XmlTextReader
Dim doc As XmlDataDocument
Dim ds as DataSet

r = New XmlTextReader("foo.xml")
doc = New XmlDataDocument
doc.LoadDataSetMapping("foo.xsd")
doc.Load(r)
ds = doc.DataSet
```

C#

```
using System.NewXml;
...
XmlTextReader r = new XmlTextReader("foo.xml");
XmlDataDocument doc = new XmlDataDocument();
doc.LoadDataSetMapping("foo.xsd");
doc.Load(r);
DataSet ds = doc.DataSet;
```

The Visual Studio.NET data designer tools can produce typed DataSets from a database or XSD schema. This enables ADO+ programmers to refer to rows inside the DataSet as if they were strongly typed objects.

The nice thing about the relationship between the DataSet and the XmlDataDocument is the flexibility it provides. You can write a single application using a single set of data, and plug it into the entire stack of services built around the DataSet (such as Web Forms and Win Forms controls, and Visual Studio.NET designers), as well as the stack of XML services (such as XSL/T and XPath). Therefore, you don't have to choose ahead of time which set of services to target with the application—both are available.

For example, data that is loaded into the DataSet via a DataSetCommand can be transformed using XSL/T by creating an XmlDataDocument and passing the DataSet into its constructor. From there, the data is treated just like any other document by the XML Framework. Of course, this process works the other way, too—the relational portion of a document can be mapped into a DataSet, which can be bound to data-aware ASP+ controls, such as a DataGrid, on a Web Form. Figure 4 depicts the complete ADO+ architecture.

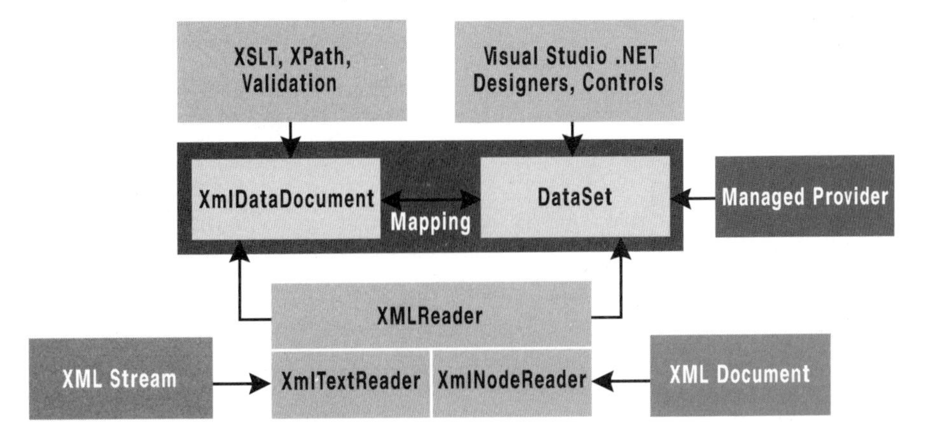

Figure 4. ADO+ Architecture

Visual Studio.NET Data Designers

Visual Studio.NET will provide rich support for designing data-aware applications. The data toolbox has design-time support for many of the ADO+ classes, including the ability to browse data sources using the Server Explorer, configure DataSetCommands using a wizard, graphically create queries, produce typed DataSets from a database or XSD schema, produce complete master-detail forms using the Data Form Designer, and much more. The data designers expose the runtime classes directly rather than having to wrap them with their own classes, as has been the case in the past. Figure 5 shows the Visual Studio.NET shell, with the query builder wizard open.

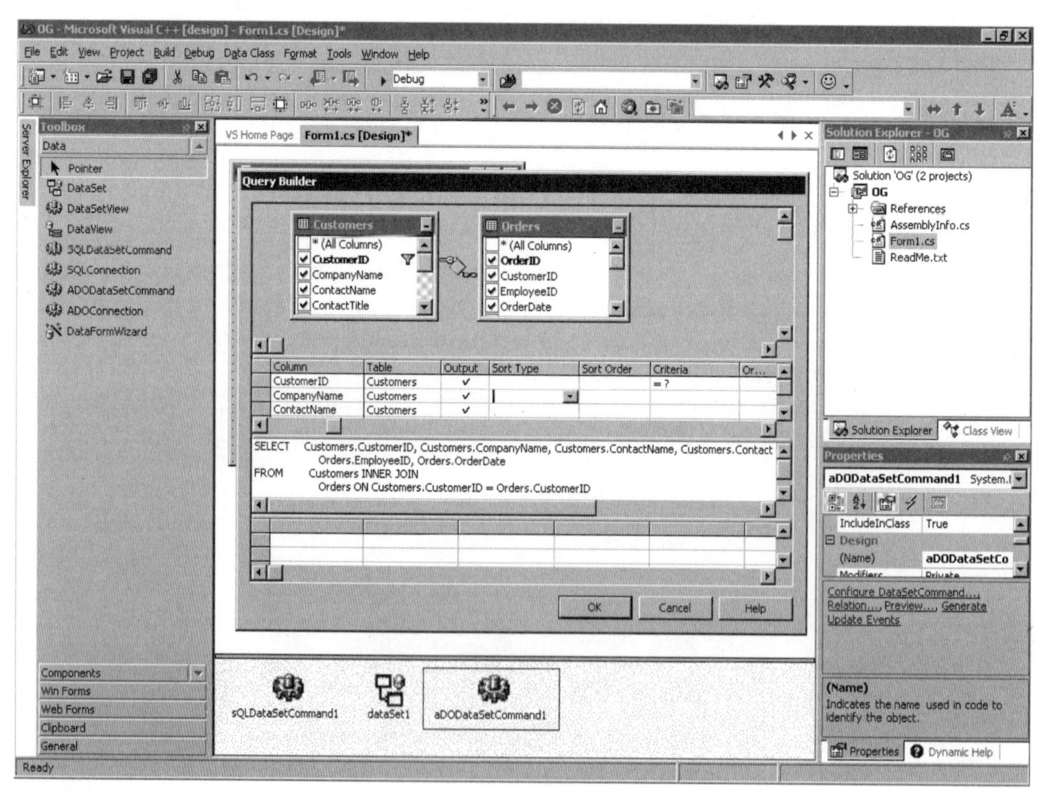

Figure 5. The Visual Studio.NET Data Designer

Typed DataSets

As I mentioned in the previous section, the Visual Studio.NET data designer tools can produce typed DataSets from a database or XSD schema. This enables ADO+ programmers to refer to rows inside the DataSet as if they were strongly typed objects, a capability that ADO programmers have often requested for the recordset. Typed DataSets are subclasses of the DataSets that are generated automatically by the data designer tool based on some schema, and they have strongly typed properties that reflect the data model of the schema. For example, accessing data in a typed DataSet that contains customers ends up looking like this:

```
'in Visual Basic
  Dim cust As CustDataRow = ds.Customers("Mike")
  Dim address As String = cust.Address

// in C#
  CustDataRow cust = ds.Customers["Mike"];
  String address = cust.Address;
```

Instead of this:

```
'in Visual Basic
  Dim cust() As DataRow = ds.Tables("Customers").Select(_
                                    "CustomerID = 'Mike'")
  Dim address As String = cust(0)("Address")

// in C#
  DataRow[] cust = ds.Tables["Customers"].Select[_
                            "CustomerID = 'Mike'"];
  String address = cust[0]["Address"];
```

The advantage that typed DataSets embody is the ability to access data using a typed class metaphor, while still being able to tap into all of the services of ADO+. Only one copy of the data exists—the data stored inside the DataSet. Thus, you can view typed DataSets as an object-view mechanism on top of the DataSet.

Conclusion

ADO+ is the .NET class framework for data access. While it stays true to its ADO roots, ADO+ also represents a big step forward. The two key enhancements are first-class support for the disconnected programming model and rich XML integration. Hopefully you have gotten a taste for what the ADO+ object model feels like; for further information, refer to the .NET Framework SDK class reference. The .NET page on MSDN® at http://msdn.microsoft.com/net has a link to the SDK download page, where you can obtain the full pre-beta redistributable. A great place to start learning more is the ADO+ section of the How-To? QuickStart, which is accessible from the main icon that is placed on the desktop after the SDK installation completes. The site also contains pointers to the .NET newsgroups where you can leave your feedback and interact with other developers interested in .NET. Have fun!

Omri Gazitt is a Group Program Manager on the Microsoft WebData team. His responsibilities include managing and delivering XML and data access technologies for the .NET Framework.

Microsoft
Self-Paced MCSE Training Kit
Microsoft Windows 2000 Server
IT Professional
Windows 2000 Professional Training Kit
Windows 2000 Network Infrastructure Administration Training Kit
Networking Essentials Plus Third Edition Training Kit

Proof of Purchase

0-7356-1445-8

Do not send this card with your registration.
Use this card as proof of purchase if participating in a promotion or rebate offer on *Web Applications in the Microsoft® .NET Framework*. Card must be used in conjunction with other proof(s) of payment such as your dated sales receipt—see offer details.

Web Applications in the Microsoft® .NET Framework

WHERE DID YOU PURCHASE THIS PRODUCT?

CUSTOMER NAME

Microsoft®

mspress.microsoft.com

Microsoft Press, PO Box 97017, Redmond, WA 98073-9830

OWNER REGISTRATION CARD

Register Today!

0-7356-1445-8

Return the bottom portion of this card to register today.

Web Applications in the Microsoft® .NET Framework

FIRST NAME | MIDDLE INITIAL | LAST NAME

INSTITUTION OR COMPANY NAME

ADDRESS

CITY | STATE | ZIP

E-MAIL ADDRESS | ( ) PHONE NUMBER

U.S. and Canada addresses only. Fill in information above and mail postage-free.
Please mail only the bottom half of this page.

start
faster
go
farther